Fishin' for Dumbasses

Fishin' for
DUMBASSES

Tips for folks who want to catch their
own food (and have fun doing it!)

John Toone

GREAT PLAINS
PUBLICATIONS

Great Plains Publications
233 Garfield Street S
Winnipeg, MB R3G 2M1
www.greatplains.mb.ca

Great Plains Publications gratefully acknowledges the financial support provided for its publishing program by the Government of Canada through the Canada Book Fund; the Canada Council for the Arts; the Province of Manitoba through the Book Publishing Tax Credit and the Book Publisher Marketing Assistance Program; and the Manitoba Arts Council.

Design & Typography by Relish New Brand Experience
Printed in Canada by Friesens
Cover illustation by Dale Cummings

LIBRARY AND ARCHIVES CANADA CATALOGUING IN PUBLICATION

Toone, John, 1974-, author
    Fishin' for dumbasses : tips for folks who want to catch their own food (and have fun doing it) / John Toone.

ISBN 978-1-926531-92-2 (pbk.)

    1. Fishing--Canada, Western. 2. Fishes--Canada, Western.
3. Cooking (Fish). I. Title. II. Title: Fishing for dumbasses.

SH571.T66 2014   799.109712   C2013-908748-6

ENVIRONMENTAL BENEFITS STATEMENT

Great Plains Publications saved the following resources by printing the pages of this book on chlorine free paper made with 100% post-consumer waste.

TREES	WATER	ENERGY	SOLID WASTE	GREENHOUSE GASES
7	3,455	3	231	637
FULLY GROWN	GALLONS	MILLION BTUs	POUNDS	POUNDS

Environmental impact estimates were made using the Environmental Paper Network Paper Calculator32. For more information visit www.papercalculator.org.

FSC
www.fsc.org
MIXTE
Papier issu de sources responsables
FSC® C016245

"Art is a lie that makes us realize truth."
— PABLO PICASSO

Thanks Dad for taking me fishing.

Table of Contents

Chapter 1

An Introduction to Fishing

Fishing as the Universal Religion

This may be your resumé…

Experience
- Survived the fugu at The Happy Sumo restaurant.
- Blistered Thumb Award for high-score on *The Black Bass* for Nintendo.
- Active as "hornyheadchub" and "commonsucker" on Plenty of Fish

Interests
- Method acting the role of Aquaman for public-access program
- Bodyscaping, spa days, anything with a loufa
- Removing water spots from the Humvee

References
- The old lady who asks "Where's the Beef?"
- The former stylist for Colour Me Badd and Mayor Sam Katz
- MC Dr. Geek from the BluBlocker commercial

Quotes
- "That's icky!"
- "Where's the nearest flush toilet?"
- "What's this plug for?"

I repeat. No experience necessary, no prior knowledge required; fishing is for you.

Fishing is for truckers and those who wear trucker hats. Fishing is for those who are indie and those who are independent. Fishing is for those who sport ironic and non-ironic versions of beards and moustaches. In summary, fishing is non-judgmental (almost to a fault). However, there are certain human qualities that lend oneself to a heightened experience. (Being a reader is a good start)

Fishing is for a man or woman of substance. (This is not a reference to the elevated levels of THC in your body). The pursuit of fish for sporting purposes has a cultural and historical weight. But you can't take yourself too seriously, because too often you will be reminded that with your skill set, you would have starved two hundred years ago. Fishing is true to you, like those before. If the fish are biting, you are in the game, and hungry for more.

Fishing is for those with refined senses. Others see a hairy shirtless blob passed out in his lawn chair, rod pointing to the sky. Others cannot grasp what is being accomplished here. They can't imagine what is on the end of your line, the hole where it dangles, the action it gives, and the monsters that circle. Fishing while sleeping is not for the beginner, and others may not recognize the practice that is required to flaunt such mastery of the art. For the act of catching is only part of the progression at play. Fishing develops a sensibility that supersedes feelings of exhaustion and intoxication. It is that powerful!

When you can start hearing quiet, after hours of fishing alone, poets hear their beat in the lapping waves at the shore, the crows' wings, and poplars croaking in the wind. Visual artists see the colours that are captured in the spots and stripes of a trout against the morning light. Musicians groove to the silence ever-changing. Sculptors find their forms in the natural surroundings. When fishing, solutions to the world's problems reveal themselves one cast a time. With each retrieve therein awaits what follows; the chance that it is something life-changing, something that can take hold and test your resistance. A lunker.

Fishing rewards creativity and experimentation. Fathers and Mothers, Grandfathers and Grandfathers, Uncles and Aunts, Brothers and Sisters, I dare you to try it on for size. Raging fires, sharp knives, and heightened sensitivity could describe your average night. What brings it to the banks is your openness to the unknown. There are creatures of the depths that can capture our imagination. If you put your hooks into them, they might drag you in. You fish, knowing the body of water holds more than you can handle. Every time you wet a line is a challenge.

Fishing can tell a lot about you. Slow down and listen to what the fish are telling you. And if you start believing all this kooky bullshit, you've been spending too much time on the water. Good on ya!

Motivational Speaking or Why We Fish

1. Meat

Value your ability to put food on the table. Recognize how handsome that fresh fish appears on the plate. Your role as provider is front and centre, not buried amongst numbers in a bankbook or exhausted from tailpipes. Prayers may not be for everyone, but we all should give pause and say thanks. Maybe those words are best found through the story of how dinner came to be. Explain the body of water, lure and landing, how the ingredients came together. This is what an adult brings to the table. Describe what it takes to feed your mind and body. These are good reasons for fishing.

Meat-lovers, eat the small fish and release the large fish. What other meat animal do we value the old and gargantuan? Conserve the best of the trophy breeding stock and encourage those genes to be passed on. When fried up all golden and such, your belly fat will increase upon sight alone. Eat what is

Mysteries of the Deep: Cam Coleman was spring fishing for walleye in current with a jig and worm tied with 8 pound test to a medium-action spinning combo. After a two-hour fight, he landed and released this lake sturgeon that measured 85 inches long with a 35 inch girth, and was an estimated 185 to 220 pounds. Aged at between 150 and 250 years old, this fish could be the oldest living thing in those parts of northwestern Ontario.

abundant and help manage so-called nuisance species. Stockpile when the bite is on, and be reminded year-round of the good fortune. Fish is fuel. It helps put on muscle.

2. Competition

I am all for competition mano-a-mano, but what does it prove when we feel the need to compete with fish? Modern battles are settled with displays of money and appearing in public with hotties. Fishing levels the playing field for the poor and ugly, for any individual who watches a fishing video and chuckles, "I could have totally reeled in that fish." Game on, you ignorant fool.

But fear not, for fishing harbours an element of beginner's luck. Perhaps beginners are more patient or their techniques novel. The inexperienced angler has a comparable chance that a fish-of-a-lifetime will strike. The experienced angler should not be discouraged, these are opportunities to reinforce your legendary guiding skills.

3. Blood-thirst

Your freezer is always full. You always keep your limit, but you don't like eating fish. I suspect the autographed photo of Relic from The Beachcombers on the wall is fake. You leave your guts at the fish cleaning station, disgusting the young family that passes by. You toss your monofilament line and it tangles up birds. You were once a contestant on Kidstreet. You equate fishing with drinking alcohol. I have zero tolerance for your likes.

How to Grab a Brain

Fishing does not require electronics. Electronics can help you catch more fish. There is more to fishing than catching fish. Don't be like most people who love to stare at screens and reflect upon their importance. Their life story is about all the things they've watched. Once, they had the decency to engage that hollow gaze in the murky confines of their home. But now, the pings and rings and cha-chings are public knowledge and top priority, for there is nothing in the present that can't wait on what the future promises.

Electronics come attached to those who bring with them a sense of urgency, because their attention is fleeting. That hunger to always be a step ahead, leaves you fighting fish while they're searching for recipes. Electronics are no substitute for experience. Learn to fish without electronics and develop your instincts, for no programmer can solve a problem so localized.

When I started fishing, the arcade was the only place to play video games. Fish finders, like cell phones, came in large briefcases. This is before we felt it our civic duty to help grow profitable companies through frivolous spending. We relied on ourselves to imagine solutions to everyday problems. (As opposed to relying on others who every day offer solutions to imaginary problems). The methods that I am about to share with you are so far advanced that they are like going back in time, for sure:

1. Wet your hands to measure water temperature. Remove from water and compare to the air temperature. It's all relative. Raise index and pinkie to determine wind direction, gauge speed, and declare your servitude to the metal gods. Beginners can use both hands.

2. Survey the horizon, take in the fresh air, and make your forecast. You may not be so perky and you'd look gauche in feathered hair, but nonetheless you qualify to predict the weather. Danger! This may involve exposing skin and exercising senses.

3. How deep? A three-count will gain additional meaning beyond your masked exploits in backyard wrestling. Conduct the experiment to measure how fast your lure falls. Hold the rod between your teeth while counting with your fingers. Those of you with missing digits might find this exercise limiting.

4. Feel the bottom through line and rod. Rocks feel hard. Sand and mud feel soft. You should feel ashamed. Inspect your hook after snags and other disruptions for further clues like weeds and wood. Do not expect to screen attractive and single mermaids with your fish finder. Save your feel for fishing.

5. Look to the skies for direction. Do not find your bearings with the device that's a fixture at crotch level. This makes you impotent. Trust maps, memory, landmarks, the sun, and what have you, but don't trust GPS.

Unconvinced, because electronics are time-savers and you are crazy busy! Without our trusty electronics, think of the effort to target suspended fish, to pinpoint the humps and drop-offs, to find a definition for thermocline, and to destroy eyesight and social graces. It could take years to catch a trophy. Yup, sure could and may never happen. Without effort, the simple rewards in life are treated as entitlements instead of accomplishments. Electronics turn the mind's eye into a reel of screen grabs and ugly feeds. Think fishing and feel the physical strain of a day on the water and envision the wilderness scene set against your rod doubled over. Appreciate what it takes to know the time without mechanical aid.

Electronics are so helpful that they free you up for other things. Ain't nothing free or freeing about the latest device. The only thing doing is fishing, and the activities surrounding such pursuits require the utmost in concentration. Handsets fall in the water, fail to perform, perform but not flawless, there's problems with coverage and power, and then there's the issue of content. The user becomes unable to perform any other function but fussing. Save your touch for the bite, and don't waste a day's fishing with pinches and keystrokes and battery changes. Quality time in the presence of nature beats another poke at the girl/boy with the alias "piercedanalfin".

Fish finders can lead you to the waters but they can't fake interest by fish. Technology is unable to distinguish whether they are active or inactive. There are fish on the screen, but why can't you catch them? This is where that fury builds and I take offence to the fish that refuses to bite my offering. I'll stay at a spot longer and go deep into my box of tricks, all the while getting myself all knotted and sour. Finally, I dismiss the false image and curse the families of the marketing executives for the fish finder conglomerate. Focus on those pixelated ones and zeros and you are counting fish before they are in the boat. Electronics ruin the secret of what is below. With every bell and whistle you become conditioned to believe that the image on the screen is real instead of a poor representation.

Try snorkeling to engage with fish face-to-face and feel what it is like to be bait. Invite yourself over and snoop around. In clear water, you can spot the white-tip of a walleye tail from fifteen feet away. Dive down and swim amongst them. Or cruise the shallows with the anticipation of being shit scared by the monster pike around the next corner. The next step is finger fishing that involves about ten feet of line and a jig without a hook and twister tail. Witness what triggers a fish to bite and note the speed of retrieve, the action, and proximity to bottom. Through snorkeling, I learned to identify the spawning beds of smallmouth bass and to slow down my retrieve and use finesse around docks and lifts.

I will concede that I like the idea of underwater cameras. It brings out the kid in you. Chances are you'll spot Flintabbatey Flonatin's golden passage to another world. For education and entertainment, have at 'er. But no device is all-knowing, and the challenge for the angler is to limit and filter this information, collect your thoughts and use good judgment. What you don't know fuels your imagination and occupies that part of your mind that needs to be kept busy while fishing.

JT's Tackle Box Essentials

1. Fishing Licence and ID
2. Needle-Nosed Pliers – hook removal, barb pinching, can be worn in a belt holster

3. Wire Cutters – with extended reach for cutting hooks
4. 8" Baker Mouth Spreader – when fishing live bait and avoiding sharp teeth
5. 9.5" Baker Hook Outs in Stainless Steel – for northern pike and treble hooks
6. 9" locking forceps with an off-set tip – for gut hooked fish and general medicine
7. Jig Head Paint Remover – otherwise you dull your hooks doing the same
8. Hook Sharpener – a small file (no batteries required).
9. Electrical Tape – small lengths for fixing the plastic bits that break too often
10. WD-40 – removes the squeaks from reels, cleans gummed spark plugs
11. Replacement rod tip – heated with a lighter and shrink fit to the offending tip
12. Fire – in the form of waterproof matches, windproof lighter, and fire steel
13. Stringer – secured with an elastic or Velcro tie.
14. Measuring tape – fabric style
15. Filet Knife – small size or folding
16. Muskol – used to make temporary tattoos with bottle labels
17. Sunscreen – SPF 30 and no Zinka tribal designs
18. Rapala Sportsman's Kit – five tools for $20

Bearded, Yet Barbless

In some places, it is illegal to fish with barbed hooks. Why? They are easier to remove from the fish allowing for a faster release. Squeeze the barbs down flat with a pair of pliers. That still leaves a little bump. If you're hardcore, use a rotary tool to grind down the barb. Recognize the insignificance of that barb in relation to your other skills and gear. It is not always about taking every stinking advantage possible. Fishing is above that. The barb doesn't affect your ability to attract or hook fish. And if you need that puny piece of metal to fight a fish...

Doug Gibson

Barbless hooks may cause you to lose a fish or two. Even more so with jumpers like bass and trout, and that leads to speculation about the one that got away. If you don't wise up after losing a fish or two, then stay off the water. The province of Manitoba keeps records of their trophy fish, and barbless hooks don't make no difference. Removing the barb from your hook is about being sporting.

When fishing with live bait, they say, the barb holds it in place. As an alternative, feed a short segment of a plastic worm onto the hook after the live bait. If you don't like the looks of that, you're probably more particular than the fish. But as chance may have it, you might have an extra plastic drink holder. Use a hole punch to create circles that will thread on the hook to retain the bait.

How lazy does fishing need to be? If you don't sweat the details, then your chance of success is reduced. Think of the technological gains in recent history, and argue that in exchange, we cannot do without the archaic mastery of the barb. I think not.

Treble hooks are nasty. They come in twos and threes on crank baits and top-water lures. They get large on the ends of pike and muskie spoons. Yes, it's an awful bother to have to remove the barbs on nine hooks per lure. And if you fish in other areas where barbs are allowed, why it's like good barbs are being put to waste. Winnipeggers hate nothing more!

If hooked, barbed lures must be pushed through, cut, and removed. This is nasty, nasty business. (Slow down and read that again). Barbless hooks can be extracted with the same fashion they were imbedded because there is no resistance from the barb.

If that isn't convincing, eventually you'll end up at the Lake of the Woods District Hospital in Kenora. Here's the drill: cut away the lure but leave the hook intact, otherwise they'll have to get invasive. Check out the display cabinet on the way to the hospital waiting room. Take your time because fishhook removal is low priority, and marvel at all the anglers before you. Upon departure, sign your lure away because fish can smell fear.

Barbs are a nuisance. When fishing man-made structures, have the confidence to get in tight knowing that you can make an easy exit with little disruption. Show some good sense to begin with, as cottager's pump water from the lake. Holes in the line and they're losing prime and that pump is labouring. Similar concerns around loons and turtles, for that odd time they chase a lure. That barb is an accident waiting to happen.

When Fishing Becomes Catching

Fishing comes natural. It is a pursuit for thinkers who reflect on their nature. Peace of mind is found in wild ideas that come from an understanding of place.

Catching is mechanical. With limited skill you can assume a position, perform a function and produce similar results. Success is a measure of size and number taken.

Fishing is sport because it is fair-chase. It rewards action, instinct and imagination. Go fishing when you need to get away from it all.

Catching has little concern for the experience or ceremony. An investment is undertaken to profit from an imbalance in supply and demand.

Fishing requires sensitivity to appreciate a day without a bite.

Catching rewards insensitivity in seeing only dollar signs.

Fishing involves food, water, and fresh air. A life's work can be shared in stories of trophies and the ones that got away.

Catching involves fuel, labour, and expenses. It is concerned with the grade of product and the channels upon which it is moved to market, pooled, and exchanged.

Fishing is a challenge. Expect more of yourself. Expect nothing of the fish.

Catching is a chore. It becomes so routine that you don't have to think about it. And the fish are expected to throw themselves at you.

Fishing is good clean fun.

Catching is good fun cleaning.

How to Get Baked – Pt. 1

Follow these easy steps, they are intuitive, and when the hallucinations intensify, borrow an eye patch and thumb it to "Margaritaville." Waste not, want not.

1. Drink only alcoholic beverages;
2. Use energy drinks or other alcoholic beverages for mix;
3. Subsist on chips, nuts, jerky, bacon, and sunflower seeds;
4. Wear no sunscreen (especially when ice fishing);
5. Apply a baby oil and iodine mixture for "bronzing";
6. Wear no shirt, only your plastic visor from Branson;
7. Smoke flavoured cigars in rapid succession;
8. Avoid sleep for the duration, be it a day-trip or several weeks;
9. Exhibit behaviours that make this fate unavoidable for others;
10. Advocate risk-taking and heavy exertion through Man Competitions.

Hot to Get Baked – Pt. 2

"Dude, like what's with the hair?"

"Dude?"

"Your hair dude, your hair!"

"Dude."

"Dude your hair is standing on end, dude."

"Dude, no. Stop laughing, dude, and take off your bandana."

"Dude?"

"Dude your hair is standing on end, dude."

"DUDE!"

Being thunderstruck is not quite the rawkus happening that AC/DC would have you believe. When you see and feel them static forces at work, dude, recognize. And get the fuck off the water now! This is of particular concern if you are in an aluminum boat and holding a rod in the air, duh. If you want *Thunderstruck* to play at your funeral man, fuckin' rights. But the irony, dude the irony, would be crushing.

Please Release Me

Catch-and-release is a skill that requires study and practice. Most anglers put all their efforts into the catching part, and underestimate the role that experience plays in a successful release. Don't be a hucker or chucker who fails to acknowledge the fish. This lapse makes fishing open for critique because of the appearance of being ignorant and cruel. Fishing is a sporting contest where the combatants can live to fight again. In Canada, 130 million fish were released of the 193 million fish that were caught by anglers in 2010. By improving how we release fish, anglers can create millions more opportunities to catch a fish each year.

Learn for yourself and consider the research. Catch-and-release is becoming politicized, so scrutinize public and private studies with an understanding of the interests at play. Question the design of the study and the degree in which these results are extrapolated to the general population.

Fishing experience is not required to be a fisheries biologist. It is fair to assume that these researchers are doing their best with the resources that they have available. Trust your instincts and be aware of the inability of science to understand and solve the world's problems. I am skeptical of any study that claims barbless hooks don't make a difference in fish mortality. Allow common sense to prevail, but always err to the side that provides the most protection to fish.

We don't know shit. Government is afraid to document the speed of change and our degree of complicity. As fisheries' budgets are slashed, anglers need to fill the void with their time and money. We need to self-initiate small changes in behaviour and fund research that is relevant to anglers. Get in front of efforts to demonize catch-and-release fishing. We can yell and scream with the rest of them, or we can tackle the issues with volunteer work and demonstrate best practices. This is my bloody opinion and here are a couple other tips:

Practise catch-and-release with particular care in the early season. Spot fish for bass on their beds, give it a fair try and give it a rest. Know when you've been busted. Avoid catching the same fish twice. Avoid the photo studio treatment. Consider the stress that the fish has gone through during the spawn. This is hard to do, because these oversexed fish are concentrated and hungry and the season has just opened. Where there are no regulations, trust your knowledge of habitat, food source, seasonal patterns and weather. If you don't have this knowledge, be prepared to defend your actions. Sportsmen know when to catch their limit and when to limit their catch.

The warmer the water, the greater the mortality of released fish. If you are fishing deep on those hot summer days, consider that you are pulling fish from 70 degree water to 90 degree air. Midday sun must hasten the drying of the protective slime on fish and cause a temperature shock from cool to hot to cool. Some fisheries can handle the pressure, but that's not the point. If you are going the fish the heat, prepare to bring home a limit and stock the freezer.

Chapter 2

The Table is Set

Butchering

In friendly Manitoba, we fail to salute our strong French tradi-tions when pronouncing the word "fillet." Instead of "feel lay," we say "fill it." If there were a colouring page of a Winnipeg boy running with a knife, the caption below would read: "Gonna fillet them pickerel!" Nope, you can't fix our stupid. However, I choose to butcher the English language to draw attention to the regional differences that give fishing its charm. Let's all resolve to tell it like it is.

Head, gut and cook 'er up, when in doubt. The meat will lift from the bones to reveal the structures you must avoid next time. Don't go at filleting blind, otherwise you'll make a mess of yourself and the fish. And you don't need me to tell you how to work a knife or draw you a picture of where the meat is on a fish. My guess is that you are already adept at searching on-line videos where raw flesh is revealed. Your job is to make the most out of that beautiful fish. Be prepared to do it all yourself, and have a plan in place to make best use of specialists and their equipment as needed.

Avoid Ralph by practising common sense when handling food. I've seen worms in the flesh of small pike caught in shal-low water during the summer heat. The more common issue with the safe eating of freshwater fish in these parts is fecal coli-form contamination. Shit happens all too often. Testing of the fish and water, not so often. Compare your catch to the risks of buying factory meat at the wholesale club, or farmed salmon, il-legal tuna, and shrimp raised in horrid backwaters. When your hands are responsible for putting the food on the table that ex-perience makes for more educated decisions.

Tastes are shaped by perceptions. Winnipeggers scoff at eat-ing fish caught from any of the city's four rivers. Newcomers must think we are crazy. Walleye migrate between the Red River and

Lake Winnipeg. Winnipeggers scarf walleye from Lake Winnipeg and boast about the demand for our fish from around the world. But you sure as hell won't catch me eating anything out of the Red River! Add the complexity of what is ethical and moral, and it surprises me that we are such an obese society.

Don't treat the fish you eat like commodities. Keep your mind open to what they can teach you about the environment and yourself. When the work is done, set aside the fillets. Take this opportunity to see what the fish was eating by cutting open the stomach. This information might help you decide between a yellow perch or crayfish pattern. I caught a trophy walleye one afternoon trolling a blue and silver plug, after finding ciscoes in their bellies at shore lunch. Food for thought...

Recommended filet knives:

· Normark with a 6" blade
· Rapala with a 9" blade

Quit Bitching and Get Into The Kitchen

Fresh fish can stand on its own without much fuss. If you have the skill set to catch fish, you have the skill set to cook. No exceptions. Apply yourself and follow these basics:

1. Prepare boneless fillets
2. Coat with the spices of your choice
3. Drench in the wet ingredients
4. Coat with the dry ingredients
5. Fry in oil.

It don't take Chef Boyardee to figure out a spice rub for fish. Use all of the following for your base: salt, pepper, onion powder, garlic powder, smoked paprika, chili powder, rosemary and thyme. Add or accentuate to taste, and consider layering flavours with the wet and dry ingredients. I tend to go heavy on the spice, because fish is somewhat bland. Don't use commercial spice mixes that have too much salt, MSG, and other creepiness.

The wet ingredients act like an adhesive and should not have too runny of a consistency. I use plain yogurt with the rind of a lemon and good squirt of juice. Buttermilk with a battered egg is a standard, and for a change, try yellow mustard or sweet chili sauce.

The idea is to cover the fillet with a thin coating. Too much slop and you'll end up with more batter than fish, and that's a big disappointment.

For dry ingredients, I turn my nose up to pancake mixes, instant potato flakes, or one of many store-bought mixes. I use a three-way mix of panko bread crumbs, corn masa flour, and whole wheat bread crumbs. Matzo meal is also a favourite, and crushed corn chips or pretzels can be used when provisions and brain cells are scarce. If you think you're something special, crush some beer nuts or candied pecans to add to the mix.

Use a deep cast iron pan and don't be stingy with the oil. The hotter you fry, the more oil that is absorbed by the food. Ignore the health police and fry your fish in lard at least once. Eat like a fur trader and enjoy a good pipe after, with a game of cards. Lard was a staple at most fishing lodges before the turn of the century. It fries fish to a crisp that should be experienced.

Switch to canola oil before the point of no return. Most prefer a light canola that allows the flavour of the fish to pervade. I recommend the natural cold pressed canola oil from T.S. Jordan of Eriksdale, Manitoba. It is liquid gold and imparts a flavour that I can only describe as sunshine. And remember you can reuse canola if you strain it back into a jar through cheesecloth and refrigerate.

The Ceremony of Shore Lunch

Use traditional sites for campfires and shore lunches. Avoid any further impact to Mother Earth. Better yet, play a supporting role by visiting often and being predictable. Clean your fish in the same spot each visit and you will feed seagulls, maybe eagles or mink, perhaps fox or bear. This applies to remote locations only, and even then do not leave your mess if there is any chance of offending others or creating unhealthy habits. And while finding your sense of place, be prepared for said party crashers. When approached by a wild animal looking for food, behave in a calm and peaceful fashion remembering that this is their home, not yours. Reflect on their good nature when they exit.

A proper shore lunch deserves the quiet side of an island. There are no waves to beat your boat against the shoreline. The island is small and it stands alone. If your fire gets away from you, this helps minimize the damage. Or if you can be trusted with an open fire on mainland, shore lunch deserves the excitement of the rapids. A soundscape and walking paths are provided.

Either way, the approach offers a sandy beach that drops off quickly; you can hit the gas, cut it, and raise the motor before you reach shore. This smooth landing equals a dignified entrance fitting for the sporting gentleperson. Feet stay dry up onto the rocky outcrops that abound. Nearby, weed beds hold pike within casting distance. Crayfish, leeches and minnows entertain the shoreline nooks and crannies. It should feel like the middle of nowhere.

Jimmy George and Michael Bailey of Norway House prepare shore lunch at Gunisao Lake.

The mixed forest is a complement of greens amidst birdsong. Stands of conifers offer shelter from the rain, and an understory of saskatoons, thickets of raspberries and pockets of low-bush blueberries help fill the void before the feast. There is a mix of sun and shade with a light breeze to keep the bugs down. Distant hinge-cut trees await for restroom improvisation. Lichen offer flashes of brilliant colours against glacial stones that are arranged for sitting and to protect the fire from wind. There may be a concave feature in the Shield rock, free of water because of a slight slope, and here the fire is cradled.

Best to get everyone involved, keep shore lunch under an hour, so you can choose to either, a) get back out on the water sooner or b) find a bed of dry moss to snooze away the afternoon. Fillet and fire are the two tasks at hand. Be brutal when you assess the skills of your lunch crew. Friends who are liabilities should look for kindling and be held responsible for cleanup. You also may want to lash a bear bell around their neck to lessen the chance of them getting lost in the woods. After removing these distractions, hopefully some competent help remains.

In the time it takes to get a fire going, the fish can be filleted and prepped for cooking. Don't go washing your fillets in the murky shallows that smell like porta-potty. Or off the transom where you just bailed the boat bottom sludge. Get your feet wet if required to find the virgin waters. Carry the fish out on the cutting board, wash and dry each fillet. Be cognizant of food handling safety and cleanliness. Cabbage leaf spotted with

algae is too avant-garde of a garnish for this crowd. Don't leave the fish in the sun.

Consider both the cooking spot and the suitability of the adjacent area for preparation and serving. Here you may experience the original granite countertop. Look for flat rock and little else that could flash up from sparks. Leave a clear area to place your pan if it gets too hot on the fire or if the food is cooking too fast. You need a draft to stoke the fire, so don't choose too sheltered of an area. Consider that you will provide a windbreak in tending the fire and food. Nice if the nearby seats are upwind to avoid the smoking section. A collection of flat and round rocks can also prove handy. Skipping stones are a bonus.

Scour the bush for deadfall that is still green. Look high and low for trees that are six to nine inches in diameter and uniform. I favour the jackpine, white spruce, or tamarack. Using a woodsman axe, cut a couple of six-foot lengths, trim any branches and smooth any knots. At the fire site, place the logs parallel to each other about twelve inches apart. Use rocks to stabilize the logs. Depending on how well the fire draws, you might prop each end with rocks or other shorter pieces. Regulate the airflow by adding or removing rocks from around the edges of these logs.

The best kindling is found on conifer deadfall that is up off the forest bottom. Snap finger-sized branches covered in dry moss of the light green or yellow variety. I call this stuff "tinderbox", realizing that makes no sense but you get the idea. Lit with newspaper, it brings a hot, fast burn with that distinct whoosh and crackle. Next add small driftwood splits about the size of chocolate bars to put down some coals in a hurry. This is not a fire of logs. Cut rounds under eighteen inches long and turn a log with a six-inch diameter into twelve even pieces. These small pieces allow you to place the heat where you need it, and maintain consistent temperature throughout your cooking time. Adjust the quantity of wood depending on the crowd, and always cut a little more than you think necessary.

If it is raining or if you are shy of kindling, use some gasoline to light the fire, but don't be an idiot. This ain't Looney Tunes, so don't pour from the gas can or make trails to ignite the blaze from a distance. Use only a cup at a time to keep the woof to reasonable levels. This is a cooking fire not a warming fire, so keep it small and contained. Fill your bailing bucket and douse any fire that creeps out of the pit.

If weather forces you to admit that you can't maintain a suitable fire, then a propane cooker with a tripod stand is the answer. For ease of transport, use the smaller five-pound tanks. You may have to buy an extended hose to keep the fuel at least five feet from the oil and flame. It's also best that the hose includes a separate shut-off valve. Don't be a cheap bastard. Buy the quality equipment or lunch will become salted minnows sandwiched between toadstools. Oil, fire and propane are a nasty mix. Stay sober or enlist a sous-chef.

You're not so much of a dumbass if you prepared the wet ingredients last night, and they somehow survived until cook time without growing life-threatening bacteria. Everything is all friendly together in a top quality freezer bag with zipper closure. Immerse those pristine slabs of freshwater goodness in there, about two or three at a time. Dreg 'em and transfer to the dry ingredients bag for the crispy layer. Before putting on the oil, be prepped and ready. It will get hot in a hurry, so be ready to plate the food and get cooking second helpings right away. A beer is good for the nerves.

An amuse-bouche is a welcome surprise for an angler still weary with boat legs. If this is all French to you, then perhaps you understand "appetizer" and "wings". Add a new first step to the filleting process. Place the fish belly up and make two parallel cuts to remove the pelvic fins and the chunk of white belly meat that lies between. If you want to get all fancy and such, these "wings" work best with Cajun or sweet chili flavours. Cook until golden and the fins turn to potato chips and the meat is rich and chewy. After a morning of fishing, you'd eat about anything. These wings may sound a bit off, but you can do worse. They also work to test the temperature of the oil.

Onions should hit the pan first. Give it a few minutes and add the potatoes. Do not use the same skimmer from ice fishing season. Keep the peel on the potatoes and appreciate the character of hand-cut versus factory crinkles. Cans of baked beans should be readied in a hobo-style, propped open and nestled into the fire. Buy small cans because they cook faster. Ignore the label that's carmelized, the BPA that's vapourized, and dare add a shot of pure maple syrup to create that *je ne sais quoi*.

Move the fillets about while cooking to ensure a golden exterior that is even, with the utmost of crisp. The fillets are half thick and half thin. Don't cook them so long as to fry that thin half to nothing. Enjoy a face full of smoke and those times crouched by the fire like others before you. Without fishing, you will never eat so fresh or enjoy that immediate physical and mental gratification. If only for one meal, experience a way of life that goes back generations. Think of how you would feel if this way of life were stolen away. Say thanks for the peace and quiet.

Field Equipment Checklist
· 20" steel fry pan with the extended handle × 2
· Stainless steel skimmer
· Woodsman Axe
· Filleting board
· Windproof BBQ lighter

- Newspaper – fire starting & fish packing
- Garbage bags – contractor grade
- Paper Towels
- Propane cooker with a tripod stand – optional
- Battery-powered chain saw – a luxury
- Salt & pepper shakers
- Tin Plates – paper plates are insulting to the fish
- Cutlery – plastic is insulting to the planet

In the Cooler:
- Ice and Beverages
- Lemons
- Hot Sauce
- Bread and Butter (in case you be skunked)
- Zippered freezer bags

Who Do You Think You Are?

Obscured behind a computer it is hard to recognize your role. Speak from experience and get outside your circles. Participate in the collection or production of food, share in the responsibility, and spend more time being active and less time being activist. Anglers and "antis" agree in protecting the natural world, agree in changing the thinking of passive consumers, and agree in voting with our dollars against factory food. Know your enemy. Fishing is something altogether different.

Fishing impacts the environment, yes. It is not a harmless activity. In the old outboard motors that spread their gasoline rainbows and the obnoxious rigs that clog highways. In the resources that go into the tons of gear designed to be disposable. It's in the pressure on the lake during a tournament. The careless that start forest fires and require search and rescue. The ignorant that take more than their fair share and then let it go to waste. It is the assholes that litter shorelines and toss cigarette butts into the water. The murderers who think excessive drinking and boating go hand in hand. The enemy is among us.

The enemy is all of us. Fruit and vegetable farms have transformed the environment through deforestation, the draining of wetlands, and the elimination of plant and animal diversity. We use the nutrients in our soils to grow corn to feed sugar to children. We have imposed our will through patented seeds, weed and pest cocktails, and yet self-control eludes us. Fishing involves the collection of wild foods. We take what's there without altering habitat or destroying other species. And it's been this way for all mankind.

But fishing diminishes the life of small animals that fall into the catch-all of "live bait". Anglers often hook live bait in ways to keep it active yet remain attached as an attractant for fish. This can mean a hook through the sucker of a leech, the upper jaw of a minnow, the clitellum of a nightcrawler, or the thorax of a crayfish. This sounds cruel. Same could be said for the deaths of pocket gophers, tiger swallowtail butterflies, and honeybees from trapping and poisoning by conventional and organic means. We can't deny our impact and we both agree it's wrong. Yet the essence of life is sacrifice. I use the bait as best I can to catch fish to eat. Farmers use inputs to maximize yields. Either way, plenty dies in the process. And, we live another day.

But when food isn't involved, any fun in fishing could be viewed as entertainment at the expense of fish. Fishing is fun whether you're catching or not. Killing is the least entertaining part of fishing. And there are limits in place to help manage our fisheries resource. Consider the widespread practice of catch-and-release. Exit interviews from the boat launch would report good times in the presence and absence of fish. Fish know nothing of being entertainers. They are consumed (literally) in nature's game of chase. And this isn't all for show.

There is fun in being a good provider. Take control of your food supply and stop paying into a system that is inconsistent with what you value in the world. Get your bearings by the fishing season. Shift your focus depending on the weather, study the patterns, and let fish shape your being. Witness the ways we compete and recognize our shortcomings. Fresh air, food and water are your baseline. Start to know a lake or section of river, and that familiarity develops into an understanding over time. Anglers are the first-responders. And this is the call of emergency.

There is pleasure in getting to know fish, like there is pleasure in getting to know all sorts of edibles. Entertainment can be found participating in the lives of others. It need not be exploitive. There is demand for meat because it satisfies human appetites. The vegan grocer has shelves of processed foods that imitate meat. For anglers, the closer we are to the action the more we enjoy and value the food we catch. Done in the presence of friends and family and when food is that fresh, it resets your spirit anew.

Animals deserve equal consideration. What makes a meal so righteous? We may share a desire to live free of pain and suffering, but it is not really our choice. I don't expect compassion or empathy from a fish, even if I were to believe that animals experience feelings and emotions. Part of the attraction of nature is that I am not safe from harm, be it mosquitoes, mother bears, and especially the unknown. I am a willing participant on their terms. Fishing engages with all of nature, not just the fish. And animals are better at living in harmony than humans. What good comes from pushing the argument to the extremes?

Going vegan makes sense if the only other choice is a Western diet of processed foods and factory meat. It's hard to disagree, if you believe a $5 Big Mac would cost $13 if the retail price included the hidden costs of healthcare, government subsidies and environmental damage related to meat production. But who the hell eats at McDonald's for serious?

Going carnivore makes sense if the only other choice is a vegan diet of processed foods and factory fruits and vegetables. The same evil empire controls large organic farms and plays god with altered versions of the patented seed and spray combinations. They fertilize with the blood, bone, and waste of animals. A uniform product is chosen for shelf life and packaged ready-to-eat. But who buys strawberries out of season?

Grandpa Toone was known for saying "all things in moderation". Yet being divisive is easier than being decisive. Polarize the conversation and you don't have to be so careful choosing your words. Avoid the grey areas, silence the balanced arguments, and the same mass of ignorant users are soon to follow. Sport fishing involves the local collection of a sustainable resource with minimal impact on the environment and a positive impact on society. Prove me wrong.

And who wants to know? PETA will make a spectacle of a young woman in a lettuce-bikini for the sake of brand awareness. They are political animals on the same moral and ethical level as any other hype business. Humans are not yours to exploit or use for entertainment. But either you are standing behind the militants or in front of them. When I stoop to new lows, it's to pick-up garbage along the Seine River. Animals notice this type of change. What we think and communicate amongst ourselves don't matter shit to them. Our minds can't control nature. We speak through our actions.

The act of buying a fishing licence may be enough to satisfy your conscience. Yet at the same time, bear witness to fisheries departments ravaged by double-digit budget cuts year over year over year in the name of austerity. Anglers respond by establishing a fund for conservation projects, and the government finds underhanded ways to claw most of that back. Dirty politics from the party that tries to brand itself as environmentalists. And at the same time, the number of licenced anglers remains steady or is increasing.

Government has no capacity to care for the environment. Their business is not forward thinking. And anglers who think they are doing their part for conservation by paying in, are missing the big picture. We need active recruitment so that volunteers can mobilize a working group to protect our fisheries. Yet again there are other forces at play.

We find the money to give each student a tablet computer. Sure, this helps to pacify the problem students. Meanwhile, consultants advise to remove swings from playgrounds. No matter, recess gets cancelled for weeks on end because of dangerous cold. We dumb down the science and math because we have enough research already. Fill their stomachs with fake food and distort their body image. These institutions are not attuned to nature, nor can they teach it. It can't be contained in four walls of red brick and neither can the will of a child. Who will teach the child to fish?

The largest animal rights organization in the world has over 3 million members and supporters. There were 3,640,926 licenced anglers in Canada in 2010. The annual revenue of PETA is about $30 million. Anglers contributed about $8.3 billion to various local economies in Canada in 2010. Now, weight your opinions.

Organize to defend our right to fish, but don't expect the government to fund the battles. We have conflicting interests. Don't wait on receiving charity status or wait for a grant to get a project off the ground. Recruit a board with a lawyer, accountant, publicist, writer, and techie. Raise cash for insurance, audit, bookkeeping, and website. Embrace new media and start the conversation with youth through technology. And kick it old school, attend those charity banquets where overindulgence leads to the purchase of wildlife-themed housewares that adorn the garage. Money alone will not sustain the tradition of fishing. We need to invest time with our children.

PETA claims that "animals are not ours to eat, wear, experiment on, use for entertainment, or abuse in any other way". There is no shame in fishing. Take pride in being stewards of our waterways and take action to ensure a succession plan is in place.

Harvest versus Kill

Say what you want, but we're only fooling ourselves. Eating meat involves killing animals. Referring to a stringer of fish, as your "harvest" sounds smug and somewhat evasive. Did you quit your day job? Did you stock those fish? Did you improve their habitat? Supplement their feed? Or did you keep the first thing that found itself on the end of your line? Harvest implies there was some thinking and doing involved in addition to finding yourself at the right place at the right time. All I know is that people overestimate their importance (me included).

Being from the prairies, I find harvest to be a loaded word. Thinking back, it imbues a sense of seasonality, rarity and tradition. Looking forward, it provokes images of factory farms, unfair labour practices and pollution. Both of these views are distorted. And killing doesn't have the greatest connotations. But I think it's wrong to adopt the language of agriculture into fishing, because of how we approach the purpose of animals. Fish are beyond our control. They are more than just our food.

Harvest is synonymous with the breadbasket of the continent, whereas fish aren't so particular as to their location. Our food should not be a single-source agreement with the big box store. What's killing the prairies is a desire to live within the city, ignorant of the farms and forest and lakes that surround. What's universal is the understanding that some are killed so that others can grow strong. Distancing ourselves from that truth is unhealthy. And so is believing that food production happens elsewhere by god who knows.

Harvest seems planned and selective. Kill seems random and rampant. Fishing can be both, and it does us all a disservice to sugarcoat. I like the straightforward nature of kill. Let us not pretend to be something we are not, like chicken fingers. Save the trickery for those who don't want to eat meat that has bones in it. These people are the real savages. Fish is not a plaything or novelty. Know what you have your hands into. Reflect upon your fish dinner and how it gives you energy. Be honest about the impact of your eating decisions. Don't mince words. Be proud of the story you tell about what you eat and how it makes you a better person.

Bring Fishing Home to Someone

Like John Lee Hooker said "nothing but the best and later for the garbage". Cook the fish up right and you can behave as you wish for the evening. That being said, standards are higher in the kitchen and the meal must be authentic. Not grubby, but true to life. Men, women, folks of all persuasions, prepare as host; don't shave, wear flannel, and curse. The fish that you caught will be infused with this spirit. Mighty tasty.

I hate to admit it, but at home I use a pancake grill. When cooking for four people, the pancake grill accommodates all the fish at once, leaving the stovetop for potatoes and extras. I live in an old house with a small kitchen. Ain't no room for extra cooktops or wall ovens or robot chefs.

I know you're disgusted, and I am ashamed at the animal that I have become (zoo animal because I'm a sell-out). Yes, I know to avoid coated cooking surfaces them being poisonous and all. But being a fisherman, I've acquired a taste for danger that I like to bring to my home-style meals on occasion. Lame excuses, you say, because the chemicals used to manufacture these products are toxic and find their way into our waters. Shame on me.

If you eat your catch once a week, you can't rely on the deep fryer alone. The pancake grill uses less oil and that equals less belly fat. The surface of a pancake grill is usually off-level so that it drains into the cup that is front and centre. For cooking the fish, we want the cooking surface to be level so that the oil

stays put. Roll a dish towel and place it under the front legs of the grill until level, or crack two beers and use the bottle caps.

Make your own breadcrumbs. Over time, collect the extras from all your breads in a freezer bag, then toast and grind. This mélange brings character and comfort to your food and magnifies the ways that you had your hands in the production.

Get the fish prepped and ready. Pile the prep dishes in the sink and clear your working and serving areas. Don't cut corners now and screw up the whole thing. Best be organized because the fish should be served hot, it cooks fast, and becomes overcooked in minutes. Choose a serving dish and line it with paper towel. This is pure illusion to placate the dieters and restore the belief that all fish is healthy.

Pre-heat the grill to 425 degrees. I use coconut oil because it gets very hot before smoking and is flavourless. And my wife says it's got that good fat. Coat the surface of the grill with the oil, and get the fish on the grill in a hurry before the oil pools and runs all nilly willy.

Be generous with the oil, adding more while cooking, if necessary, and at the halfway point.

If you cook the fish for the same amount of time on each side, it will be difficult to get that double deep crisp without overcooking the fillet. Start with the curved side of the fillet face down (skin side up). Cook the first side a minute or two longer. You will notice the fish cooking along the edges and before it progresses more than a half-inch towards the centre, flip. This side will be served face up on the plate. I don't like hitting it with lemon juice until it is off the grill, otherwise that's more poached action.

Walleye is the fish of the traditional Canadian shore lunch. As the youngster in camp, I earned my place amongst the men by working the bucket of fish heads. Using a smaller-sized fillet knife or even the caping knife from your hunting kit, make an incision along the cheekbone. Work the flesh away from the bone and pull the meat from the skin with your thumb. That's a half of one bite. You need a big camp and a mess of medium-sized fish to justify the fuss, but it's a waste of good eating otherwise. The rich flavour and hearty texture has earned this delicacy the name "freshwater scallop" or in some places "pickerel cheeks". Fix 'em blackened Cajun-style or with butter, wine and herbs.

If fish were steak, serve it medium. Often there is a stray piece of fish to be found amongst the filets. Use this as your tester piece, flake at its thickest, and look for hints of gray or translucence near the center. Do not cook away all the juices. I repeat: do not cook away all the juices. When the tester piece reaches medium, enjoy the bon mot. You don't serve a steak all carved up, and fish deserves the same care in presentation. Keep it together.

Gear & Stuff

· George Chuvalo Grill (bootleg Canadian version of the popular American grill)
· Cabela's 14" Cast Iron Deep Skillet
· Two-sided spatula
· Brush to move the oil

Chapter 3

How to Catch Fish

Approaching the Body of Water – 4 Step Program

1. Follow the Masses

Question this as wisdom lest you find yourself ordering the toy meal from a fast food restaurant inside a big box store. Too much of that evil in the world already. In fishing, if they ain't catching then they be moving on. Spend some time around the water, count bodies, and soon you will realize the hot spots. But that may only tell you where the fish were, not where they're at. Try following the retired folk. They get the choice spots because they're up before the birds. And if you can't hear them complaining from a hundred yards off, they're catching. However, these creatures of habit are also nostalgic, and the last time this spot produced could have been when chaps courted dames with Studebakers. Following the masses is a strategy much like tossing coins into a wishing well.

First come, first serve is the rule. Muscle in when the opportunity arises but expect poor sports, and in response practise your etiquette. Be honest when asked if you've caught any fish. Don't hide your lure, be evasive, or get grapefruits under your arms when someone gets within a rod-length. There is no "locals only" policy. Treat fellow anglers with respect, don't bring a flatdeck of gear and pretend you know shit. I don't care if you're Bob Izumi's personal sommelier, and the fish couldn't care less. Be friendly and don't get your back up. It's never as easy as it looks. Fishing is about the experience, not keeping up with the masses or protecting turf.

2. Sense and Sensibilities

As you come up on the stream, it sounds like the flutter of excitement in your belly. You see fish surfacing, you smell rot, you

taste insect. Duh, it's fish fly season. Beyond the obvious, become attuned with your environment and the aquatic environment by extension. Check the idiot box or leave the confines of your home to determine the temperature, barometric pressure, moon phase and hours of sunlight. Don't blow a gasket trying to process it all. Build an awareness of how these variables affect fish activity. Train yourself to think first then act.

Start with visuals like a steep-banked shore or island. Imagine the transition spots or pinch points between two features. Spot and fish cabbage beds, overhanging trees, and man-made structures that provide shade and hiding. Creeks and springs add nutrients to create cover. Look and be amazed at what's out there when you stop to notice. In clear, shallow waters, consider how light availability and water temperature influence the movement of fish throughout the day. Find a vantage point and use polarized glasses to spot fish or bait.

In muddy waters, fish rely more on smell and taste to find food. Fishing bait in current produces scent trails that can bring fish to you. If the law allows, you might take this further and chum the waters with vile concoctions of meat and grains. Yet if nothing's doing, then like pissing in the wind, you're all wet and half-empty. So try to imagine how the current has shaped the river bottom and how patterns of erosion influence water clarity and structure. That sounds like high school science, so let's dumb it down to a more appropriate level: fish the slack waters on the outside of river bends. If that makes no sense, maybe there is hope. If one proceeds on feel alone, then they are vulnerable to bullshit. Pay attention and now apply the information your receptors have collected.

3. Stupid is What Stupid Does

Where to begin? Not gonna catch a damn thing if y'all ain't fishing. Hit the road and take the shotgun approach: a game of luck and instincts. Be methodical at each stop, cover the water with fan-casts, work a handful of different lures, vary your retrieve, and only then move to the next spot over. Efficiency can be improved by pre-rigging two or three distinct rod, reel, and lure combos and then cycling through. Or still-fish with a rod holder or slow drift with a bobber, while casting with another rod for more active fish. Obey the rules on the number of rods allowed and your proximity to each rod. Bring along the kids and maximize your chances at that first fish.

In the meantime, what are you pulling in? Get a feel for bottom and the snag situation. Hold onto your wallet. If you don't find fish, you will find weeds and whatnot. Vary your casts until you pinpoint the edges of the weed beds. Then slow down your presentation and be ready for the subtle bite. If your snags suggest a rocky bottom, move to floating rigs or dial in a crank bait.

Don't just keep throwing the same hardware out there without thinking of ways to remedy any lack of action. Same goes for sexual relations.

When you attract that first bite, make a mental note of how you worked it, and keep fishing hard all the same. Dwell on a fish that you missed and that anger becomes a distraction. Land your first and assess what you did and what you didn't. Admire the fish and learn the variations in colour that are unique to each body of water. Walleye, for instance, can range from grey to green to golden. That sun-bleached look comes from shallow waters, the olive tones from weed beds, and that golden colour from deep water or muskeg nearby. At least that's my experience in Manitoba lakes. To improve on trial and error, formulate fishing experiments that manipulate a few variables. Then log your progress, analyze the results and draw conclusions. If it helps, complete your science fair project with a triptych of crayon sketches on cocktail napkins under the heading "How Jagerbombs Make Me Green". And nerd, prepare for shoulder punches, ear flicks, noogies and surf shorts.

4. Hit the Books

Find a bottom-contour map for the body of water you are fishing. Look for those featureless areas, and in doing so, eliminate a good portion of the lake from your game plan. Next, note the areas with dramatic transitions like the steep drop-offs where those contour lines bunch up. Of particular note are deep holes that are close to shore. Don't forget the high points as well, like shoals, sunken islands, humps, points and what have you. These spots hold fish and also the bottom-ends of many boats and motors.

Mark the obvious structure and then take a step back and consider the inflows and outflows. For Shield lakes, I like to imagine the lay of the land continuing below the water's surface.

Channel markers and navigation routes also indicate areas where the structure isn't obvious. If you fancy yourself a sleuth, scour historical records for locations of old commercial sites, wrecks, and transportation routes. Next best thing is scuba diving.

Relive your high school years with the following science gems:

1. Faster water is found on the outside of turns of rivers. Erosion takes place, steep drop-offs result and fine sediment is held in suspension.

2. Slower water is found on the inside of turns of rivers. Deposition takes place, creating a more gradual drop-off of gravel with sand on top.

How does this apply to fishing? Hell if I know. My scientific knowledge became stunted when I discovered shot-gunning beers. Point being: admit when you are in over your head and avoid getting there in the first place.

Aquatic vegetation influences seasonal patterns that are predictable year over year. Too complex? Weed man, locate the weed. Plants produce oxygen, provide habitat for insects, attracting baitfish, and that brings in the bruisers. Mark the beds and the time of year they were productive. Veg don't move too much over time, unless an invasive species enters the lake. I like lily pads for northerns and bass, and cabbage for walleyes. Shallow bays will become choked when that hot weather hits and the water gets warm. Consider how the sun's position can create shaded pockets amongst clumps of tall cabbage. Fish these areas like you hunt a forest; working the breaks in cover and staging areas near to the food source. And this be irie mon.

Now come full circle, and follow the masses but with intelligence and an end goal in mind. Allow that old-timer back into his hot spot, and chances are that he'll share a few secrets after telling a few stories. Treat this as a reconnaissance mission, but never go so low as to cast over someone to check their lure. Use tact, ask questions and be an active listener. Focus on the tackle box and allow small talk to beget a show-and-tell session. Overall, approach the water aware of what's out there, but accepting of its mysteries. Fools jump in without an understanding of the pitfalls. Use your head and wear a lifejacket.

Luring without the Internet

Practice by tying one on each day. Master that skill so you don't think twice before changing lures every fifteen or twenty minutes. Select your lure based on a realistic assessment of the fish available and your skill set. Go after the most abundant species and don't buy a lure unless you are committed to learning the technique to make it work. Build your tackle box over the years, not with one shopping spree. (Get off the bandwagon you trier). Specialize at first in spoons, jigs, and live bait rigs.

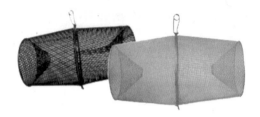

Become a trapper and catch whatever swims, slithers or crawls. This is your lure. No decision making required. I like the two-piece, torpedo-shaped traps with openings at each end and a spring clip that you attach to a rope. If you lose a band member and find yourself with an extra plastic jug, you can make your own trap in the downtime. However, if you invest a twenty spot in quality, you might get forty plus years out of your trap like I have.

In the olden days, traps were made of glass. The new ones have a black, vinyl-dipped wire frame. Buy at least two, because others will want in on the action. Add the flash of tin foil or re-use an old spinner for attraction. Or drill holes in an old film container and pack it with cat food of a fish variety. Same variables at play as amusement parks, bakeries, and strip clubs: follow your nose, indulge in what you find, feel trapped.

Recognize that dudes are making their own lures and offering them for sale to other likeminded dudes. Jig heads that have been custom dipped to keep the paint out of the eye. Plugs made from balsa and painted with an artist's brush. Tackle that you earn when you learn how to avoid and free snags. Dudes might otherwise be painting fire tiger front-ends on Dudettes' mini-van. It would be culture shock to lose that, but nevertheless, support dudes that take it to the next level by bring it back to the basics. And if this is your thing, take up fly fishing. Hard to beat catching smallies on the surface with deer hair poppers that you tied. Done that.

Enough of the rambling prose and exhausting detail; now figure this shit out for yourself:

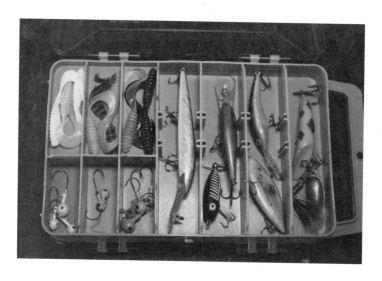

Food Source	Colour Match
Ciscos and Shiners	White, black, gold, silver, blue
Perch	Fire tiger (orange, green, yellow and black)
Worms	Brown, olive, pumpkinseed
Leech	Black, purple, olive
Crayfish	Brown, orange

Clear Water and Sunshine

Use the sun's reflection to advertise the crippled minnow lunch special. Try plastics that sparkle or hammered metal blades that wobble and flash. Choose lures that stay true when trolling with lots of line out. Fish get skittish in these conditions.

Murky Water and Overcast

Less light penetration suggests that you bump up the colour into the unnatural realms of chartreuse and orange fluorescent. The fish will rely less on sight and more on scent and sound. Add a rattler or vibration, to trigger a reaction from a fish's lateral line sense.

Active Fish

Troll a plug with rattle to locate fish willing to chase a fast-moving lure. Use marker buoys and focus on the active fish with casts or jigging. Enjoy it while it lasts, avoid being patient, and troll on to locate the more active fish when the bite slows.

Inactive Fish

Invite a taste by finessing soft lures spiked with scents or attractants. A marabou tail with tinsel lends further action to a retrieve that employs a spastic twitch. Or slow that spinner bait or spoon right down and size up to entice a fish to expend energy.

Deep Water

Don't matter whether it's two-toned, tiger stripe, or sparkle fleck as the spectrum tightens up more around the blacks and greys the deeper it gets. Create vibration with lures that imitate minnows or live bait rigs with spinners and beads.

Shallow Water

Go weed less if you're working the area between surface and bottom. I like fat plugs that dive a few feet and then float back up to the surface. If you think you are awesome, learn how to walk the dog with a Zara Spook.

Hot Water

Slow troll or drift live bait rigs with enough weight to keep your lure down deep. Stretch out those nightcrawlers and leeches, give the fish lots to chew on, and bury a stinger hook. Use a floating Lindy rig to keep the bait off bottom even with the slowest presentation.

Cold Water

Enjoy the versatility of grubs with twister tails. Cast, jig and troll to locate the active fish. Use premium grubs impregnated with scents or tip your jig with a live minnow for extra movement.

Calm Water

Use surface plugs and oddities like the duckling for muskie or grasshopper for bass. Rip a spinner bait along the surface so that upper blade is slapping and dancing about. Choose lures for casting and avoid spooking fish with loud motors, loud mouths, and worst of all, loud motor mouths.

Choppy Water

The wind stirs the silts and aquatic insects creating conditions similar to murky water and overcast. Move to the shallows and run diving crank baits until you find the depth where the fish are feeding.

Small Fish

Don't limit yourself just to small fish. Use spinners and spoons to give the appearance of something larger. Consider the size of the hook more than the size of lure. Think of all those fat trout with nasty jaws biting little dry flies and nymphs, but that's more about presentation than lure selection.

Large Fish

Go big to catch big but only if you have the rod and reel combo to manage the extra weight. Buck tails add bulk and action to spoons and spinners. Cut bait like goldeye or frogs have the scent power to bring in channel cats.

Catch your first fish and adjust your plan of action. Fly fishers will use a stomach pump and knowledge of insects to choose their lures. It seems kinda heavy to fight the fish and empty its belly. Best to inspect the stomach of a fish that you filleted for dinner. Stick with what is working, but try to isolate whether it's the lure, presentation, or dumb luck that's causing the bite.

Above all else, don't overdo it. Less lures = smaller tackle boxes. Don't allow your insecurities to be exposed through the rampant consumption of oversized items. Too much tackle limits your ability to hike into spots or fish from a canoe or kayak. Fly-in fishing trips always have weight restrictions, so best learn to make do with the basics.

Dragged out Kicking & Screaming

Drag helps tire fish by providing resistance on the line being pulled from the reel. Drag that is set too loose will result in over-playing the fish and wasting the energy of all involved. Drag that is set too tight, will result in your line failing and in the backlash, you falling ass-over the gunwale. Best to err to side of your drag being set too loose. Be familiar with the operation of your reel before the need arises and you can adjust your drag on the fly, a half-turn at a time until the battle turns to your favour.

If you want to be all uppity, the first time you set your drag, find a fishing partner to help. Spool your line, take the free end through the rod guides, and tie it to the end of a fish scale. Have your partner hold the fish scale, you increase pressure on the rod,

and when the drag engages note the weight reading on the scale. A good starting point is to set your drag at 25 percent of the break strength of your line. For example, the drag on a reel spooled with eight-pound-test should engage at two pounds of pull, duh.

I like to do things myself, so I adjust my drag by feel. My setting is probably closer to 40 percent of the break strength of my line, and I got there by making small adjustments while fishing. Tie-on a jig head and imbed the hook into the edge of a wooden dock. Stand back and horse on the rod to get an understanding of the force required for the drag to engage. Get a feel for the tension that is held in the rod and reel and their capability to hold up without giving line. How will you manage when fighting the fish of a lifetime? Know your limitations and the limitations of your equipment.

Marketing aside, the price of a reel should reflect the quality of the drag system. Spend more for drag that is smooth, consistent, and durable enough to fight a lunker without bursting into flames. This is a function of the material and craftsmanship of the discs that are used to create resistance. The drag knob or star-wheel should be positioned in a place that seems intuitive and should offer audible clicks or detents to assist in adjusting the drag while fighting fish.

Check your drag before each day on the water so that there are no surprises. Braided line is so strong that if your drag is set too tight, the reel and rod might fail. You've been warned. A light action rod has more flex than a heavy action rod, and you might run a somewhat tighter drag setting because of the rod's ability to absorb the pressure of the fight.

The Mind is a Terrible Thing to Waste

Feel confident that you will land a fish. Rely on your education, despite knowing the popular school system neglects 90 percent and fails the other 10 percent. For these institutions excel in putting asses in chairs and creating low expectations, both keys to an enjoyable fishing experience. Schooling teaches waiting for no good reason and this sharpens reactions to bell stimulus. Preparedness involves quieting the chaos, occupying the mind, being impervious to insults, and performing the occasional simple task. The pursuit of trophy fish is a feat of endurance not unlike surviving school. Imagine an outdoor classroom where peace and quiet clears the mind, while fishing engages the senses. In conclusion, teach a man to fish and feed his body and mind for a lifetime. And school sucks. And prepare to be schooled.

Cast the First Stone

You may be a danger to yourself and others. If so, practise casting with a squash ball, half-ounce lead weight, or with the boy band action figure you keep bedside. You will graduate to a hook when you can demonstrate that you can put one out where you intended without subjecting yourself and others to body modification.

Perhaps, this learning experience is best reserved for the privacy of your own backyard. Or, don't give a damn what other people think (assholes, all of 'em), don the tracksuit and visor, and jaunt over to the nearest park for land fishing. If anyone asks your problem say "When I catch the leprechaun, I will wish you dead". That'll fix 'em. Beware of aggressive birds and squirrels.

When ready for water fishing, first check the fine print on the rod for the range of lure weights that the manufacturer recommends. Stay within the range or risk the safety of all mankind. A mismatch results in a pathetic cast and a reel inclined to bird's nest. There is no whip to heavy rod when casting a light lure. A light rod will stress and lack control over a heavy lure, and then that light rod will wag like a dog's tail during the retrieve. Find that balance or you won't know what bit you. In summary, listen to the maker.

Next, note the position of the lure in relation to the tip of your rod. I recommend that you leave about twelve inches of line between your lure and the end ring of the rod. If you reel up too far, you lose distance and the hook might get all caught up in your rod, fouling your line. If you reel up too little, you lose control and the hook might get all caught up in your ass. Find the sweet spot and maintain enough of a connection to the lure to place your casts, while using the slack to accentuate the whipping action of the rod.

For a spinning reel, align the bail so that the line roller faces up. Take the line in your finger and flip open the bail. The line should rest in the middle of the pad of your index finger. This allows for a controlled release that will not inhibit the forward motion of the line.

For bait-casting reels, depress the button or thumb bar and hold it down during the back cast. After the release, feather your thumb over the line as it spools out to reduce the occurrence of bird's nests.

After the cast, pause before closing the bail or starting to reel, to allow the lure to sink to the bottom. With spoons, spinners, and jigs a fast retrieve will bring it closer to the surface and a slower retrieve will keep it near bottom. You can use a countdown technique if your casts are going to deep water and the fish are suspended from bottom.

Know the limits of your casting ability and position yourself to cast beyond your target without herculean effort. Find a pace that you can maintain all day. If you can keep your target within easy reach, your arms and back won't be rubber by the time the big one strikes. Place your casts parallel to structure to maximize your time in the strike zone during the retrieve.

If you see a fish jump, don't always cast to the splash. Scan the water for signs of a food source (bugs or minnows?) and try to anticipate the next point of attack.

Sidearm Toss

Your rod moves along a horizontal plane at waist-level. Face your target and bring the rod to your side. The range of motion should cover the five o'clock to two o'clock positions. Start with both hands, and then switch to one hand as you become proficient. Learn to time the release of the line or thumb bar so that the lure lands in the direction you are facing.

This is basic cast that is fit for short to medium distances. The lure is always visible and away from your body to avoid the unpleasant version of a hook-up. You'll need a large footprint to accomplish this cast, so it is not recommended for crowded docks or combat fishing.

Overhead Power Cast

Your rod moves along a vertical plane, with the back-cast stretching overhead. The range of motion should cover the two o'clock to ten o'clock positions. Release too soon and the energy of the cast takes your lure up amongst the seagulls. Too late, and the abrupt splash in the water announces that amateur hour has begun.

This intermediate cast is fit for medium to long distances. Maximize the whip of your rod but do not overextend your back cast. Be mindful of what is behind you.

Underhand Pitch

For this cast, your rod also moves along a vertical plane, but you bring the rod tip down instead of reaching back behind you. Rest the bait in your hand, drop the tip of the rod and swing the lure forward with a pendulum motion. Use this cast as a finesse move or shoot it harder to skirt under branches that extend over the water.

This intermediate cast is fit for short to medium distances. It's a quick way to cover water and work heavy cover like trees and man-made structures. The underhand pitch also works when a fish follows up but does not strike before the end of the retrieve. Since your rod tip is already down, use the pitch to make a short, quick cast while the fish is still interested.

Flipping

This cast is similar to the underhand pitch, but instead you work with a fixed length of about nine feet of line. Open the bail and take the lure in hand. Add to the length of your fishing rod with an arms-length of line to start. Close the bail. Use your off-hand to adjust the length of line required for each cast. Establish a rhythm and maintain that pendulum motion. There's no need to take your lure in hand with each cast. Flipping harkens back to the days of cane poles with string.

Flipping works best in ambush points along undercut banks or in weed beds with less than six feet of water. This up-close and personal approach allows you to work pockets and crevasses in detail. As with the underhand pitch, flipping benefits from a longer and stiffer rod (7 foot plus, medium-heavy action) that has the backbone to rassle them fish out of the thick of it. Use a line that is low-stretch, resistant to abrasion, and has a 25 pound test equivalent. In these parts, you need a solid hook set plus the pulling power to keep the fish from wrapping that line around a tree.

Rod Holding for the Inexperienced

At least half of the adult population should already have this task in hand. Many others have demonstrated that they are also well-practised in this regard. One could conclude there is a body of knowledge.

To improve upon what you know, trying placing your finger on the rod blank to feel changes in the action of your lure and/or those sensitive bites. Some manufacturers expose the blank in the handle and bring it through to the butt-end of the rod. Detect those light taps of a fish in close and be ready when it gives that one long pull.

Extend this idea to placing a finger on the line. This comes natural when flipping, but also borrows from the light touch required when fly fishing. When jigging with a spinning reel, try moving your hand forward and taking the line up with your finger. Detect those slight tugs and feed that extra line to the fish so they feel no resistance.

In general, the idea is to cradle or balance the rod and reel across your fingers instead of using a death grip, death clutch, or the dreaded claw of Baron von Raschke. But maybe you've already learned that the hard way.

For Life's Snags

Test your bait before you start fishing to check that it is running true. Think about the action of the bait and adjust to any changes during your retrieve. Assume that any interruption is a fish, until you discern otherwise. Never let down your guard. Aquatic vegetation will feel like a soft tug. Give your bait a quick jerk to free it. If you feel the bait stop dead, consider this might be a snag before burying the hook in a log. Don't allow wishful thinking to force that hook set when you know bloody well that wasn't a bite.

Set the hook and feel for that energy on the end of the line. Freeze for a moment with that rod tip up and flexed. Do not reel but keep everything under tension. Look where the line meets the water to sense any movement. Apply more pressure on the lure and try to steer it from where it seems stuck. Take the rod back another notch, not like a double hook set, but more a twitch to be certain that a big old monster is eating in his sleep. After a few seconds of this dance, admit the snag that you are in, note the position for future reference, and analyze potential causes. Branches might feel like they have some give, while rocks do not. Branches break, while rocks do not.

Great force is not required when freeing snags. Work slack line to create a whipping motion that might disentangle those pesky trebles. Try reeling the line taught and then taking up an arms-length, like you would if you were flipping. Create the maximum amount of tolerable tension and then spring it with a quick release of that line. Move about to create different angles, and try pulling in all directions. As a last ditch, give it slack and let current or wave action work it free while you sulk.

Caution is required when trolling with braid line, especially in the fog of digestion after a substantial shore lunch. Depending on the speed of travel and intensity of snoring, lines and rods can break before there is a chance to react. Use spinning rods, and be ready to reach over and flip the bail if necessary. This is also where a bait-running reel comes in handy.

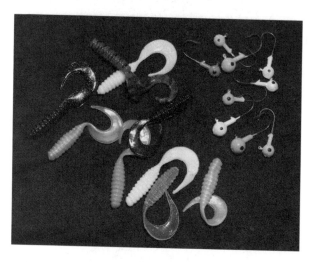

Lures can be replaced and fishing time is often more valuable. To break off the lure, grab the line with your hand, turn your body and pull away. The odd time the snag pulls free because a hook breaks or bends, so watch yourself. Don't point your rod tip at the snag and walk backwards, as this stresses the rod and drag system. Don't cut the line as this can leave long lengths to get in a tangle. After any snag, remove about five feet of line and re-tie your lure. Inspect and sharpen hooks. And don't forget to place your lure somewhere different next time.

The Jig is Up

As teenagers, many become well practised in the motion that is characteristic of jigging. In fishing, an approach that is heavy-handed or brutish will prove less successful. Try a nice light twitch, the slow and steady swim, or something out of the ordinary. Variations abound from the basic up and down, so look for inspiration in the rhythms of poetry, wind chimes, beer chugging and intercourse. The only proviso is to keep in touch with your lure at all times. Any slack gives fish the opportunity to snatch your bait undetected. And tone down your presentation, stop and start, so that the old and weary fish have their chance. Consider that waves can create enough movement to get a good jig going without the angler having to be awake. This is an advanced technique.

More often than not, the jig is on or near bottom. Small rocks with the odd glacial erratic require persistence and good hands. Find ways to creep up and over boulders, and to develop enough sensitivity to twitch your way out of snags before compounding the problem with a hook set. On sand or mud bottom, work the hard drop to stir things up. Drag bottom and tick the rod while the lure rests in place to create movement in the twister tail or tube skirt.

Fish may strike on the up-pull or the down-drop of the jigging motion. At the best of times, your lure might not hit bottom between fish. When you sense fishy activity, provide no resistance until the fish gets that hook into their mouth. Rule out a snag, by checking where your line meets the water and noting if the line is moving in one direction or another. The hook set when jigging should be fierce. Reel down to maintain tension, and sweep up with a hard snap.

Refine your technique, if the fish are biting but you're skunked and seem late on the hook sets. You find your bait

stripped or ripped in half. Bait-running is an intermediate technique for when the fish are sluggish, or that leech or night crawler may be such a mouthful that it requires some maneuvering. A bait-running reel has a secondary drag system that buys you some time while keeping at the ready. Flip a switch to allow the fish to take line with little resistance. Flip the switch back or turn the handle to set the hook. Accomplish the same without a specialized reel, by opening your bail by hand and feeding the fish line with your fingers. Do not attempt unless you have enough experience to avoid gut hooking.

When there are light winds, I prefer drifting in a boat with the motor off. Have a good listen to nothing and think about how good that sounds. Drift the same area at least a few times but with some variation in your approach each time. You want to make sure the fish are seeing your bait if they are inactive. To shuttle around, an electric trolling motor is boss. An electric trolling motor that is foot and remote-controlled and guided by GPS is Big Boss Man. Oars and a paddle also work. They are made of wood, they float, are rugged, require no power source and are inexpensive. Your choice.

Use a marker float to give you a visual reference for the start of your drift. Use another at the end of your drift, and use the others to mark bites or fish. Dare to avert your eyes from a screen and look out across the water. Read the islands and shoreline for clues about the structures that build up to the water's edge. Imagine in three-dimensions the bottom contours and vegetation that connects points of interest. Only then, use electronics to help shape that perspective.

Marker floats are cheap to buy, but as a Winnipegger, I can't help but dispense advice on being thrifty. Rummage a recycling bin for four plastic bottles that are bright in colour. Attached fifty feet or more of sideline and a 4 to 6 ounce weight to each bottle. Don't forget to pull your floats from the water when your fishing day is through.

Trolling Without the Internet

Manthers and cougars bait each other with similar techniques in drinking establishments. Their rituals involve strutting feathered mullets and reenacting scenes from *Dirty Dancing*. Concerning fishing, trolling involves a methodical approach to determine the depth, speed, and path of travel that will put you on fish. Troll to cover water and locate active fish. Get that lure in the strike zone and offer the fish a fleeting chance at an enticing meal. Target fish that are on the chase, instead of the old sit-and-wait routine. Take it to them.

Troll humps and drop-offs to work schools of walleye. Fish the chop (rough water) using a combination of drifting and trolling. This dance involves much attention and skill to keep lines taut and to make the most of each successive pass. Start with live bait rigs fished near bottom and don't be too jumpy. Consider your speed and the size of bait, and give the fish some noshing time before the hook set.

Be aggressive and troll the edges of weed beds for northern pike. Stop and start to allow those in the bow to cast into the deep cover as opportunities arise. Or be passive and troll shore-lines taking in the scenery. Fish steel leaders with flashy spoons, and be ready for weary trophies that follow-up to the boat. When they are close enough to look you in the eye, be cautious not to set that hook up in your face. Instead, keep the bait in the water and turn large figure-eights with the rod. Hold tight.

Troll with what your mother gave you. But if you're par-ticular, a trolling outfit starts with a more substantial rod of the 6 foot 6 inch to maybe 7 foot 6 inch variety, with a solid back-bone and a light tip. Add a large reel for balance and for line capacity when working the depths. Larger reels also move more line with each turn of the handle. And thus saves you the embar-rassment of an over-muscled reeling arm (#1 plastic surgery for professional anglers). For extra punch, I prefer 12 or 15 pound test monofilament, but braided line with a fluorocarbon leader may be a better recommendation. If you are targeting suspended fish, add a line counter to the reel and bring consistency and dis-cipline to your game.

A rod holder for trolling makes a sweet addition to a canoe or kayak. With your line in the water, move with stealth into haunts that no others vessel can navigate. But first practice the hook set, fight, and landing plans, or you might end up all wet. Uncoordinated folk should be fitted with keyhole lifejackets and water muscle anklets. Best to add a paddling partner, picnic bas-ket, and herein is the essence of fishing – simplicity, silence, and brilliant execution.

Powerboats often travel too fast for trolling even at their lowest forward speed. You can adjust the idle on the motor, use

a lower pitch prop, or attach a trolling plate, but that might not be enough if you're rocking a 150 horse or more. Motor tweaks might also affect the control, top speed, or revs. If you've got some big fancy boat, have the good taste to shut down that gas-guzzling ruckus, go electric or use a kicker motor. Long-shafts and tiller control will keep you nimble.

If you're bush, slow your troll by dragging slop buckets from the boat. First hold up your pants and then combine the lengths of rope that were your belts. Attach two slop buckets and tie them rigs off on the doorknobs that you use for stern cleats. The drag of the buckets will help slow your progress. More refined versions involve straps and fabric bags with a weighted bottom and floating top. Use said devices in pairs and they can also help control and stabilize the boat rough water.

If conditions permit, another way to slow the boat is to troll in reverse. The added bonus is that the lines are kept away from the propeller. This is a trusted technique when you have three or more people in a 14-foot aluminum boat fishing plugs with trebles. Reverse mode does sacrifice comfort and boat control. In rough water you're eating waves on the back troll. Make splashguards by clamping pieces of Plexiglas to the transom on each side of the motor.

Trolling rewards the multi-tasker who can captain the boat and wield the rod and soak it all in. To start, note the action on the tip section of your rod when your lure is running true. Any variation during the troll could indicate a strike, weeds, or bottom. Pitch the bait out the side of the boat and free-spool. Bells and strike alarms can be used if you find yourself overwhelmed.

The more line let out, the deeper the lure will dive. To locate fish, start at the shallow end of their range. With each unsuccessful pass, drop your lure a couple of feet deeper. Sunlight and boat traffic tend to push fish down as the day progresses. Pay attention to the bend in your rod to gauge the speed of your presentation.

Be aware of what's left on the spool. You'll need some room to give when you hook up a fighter in the depths. Don't fish beyond your means. The amount of line you have out in the water can affect your reaction time to the strike. That length also magnifies problems with line stretch when working through cover.

Trolling invites you to add more lines in the water, as many as the law allows. A large spread can be managed from a single boat, though frustrations with tangles can bring trouble to a beauty day of fishing. From the simple to the spendy, trolling can be improved with Dipsy and Jet divers, planer boards, and downriggers. Fish can be spooked by the intrusion of the boat and motor, and might avoid the resulting path of your lure. Planer boards and Dipsy divers work your lures down and your lines out the port or starboard. Downriggers are for big water and serious fishing. Troll on.

Bite Me

I can assume that you are well versed in "Whoot, There It Is", and perhaps also "Whoomp! (There It Is)". When fish let it drop, their bite is often not so pronounced as to incite booty shaking and poetic licence. Do not be discouraged, for you will get to know the tap tap and the thump of a fish, and in their absence, you will learn to watch the line for movement. With each bite, collect intelligence for future reference and summons that muscle memory. Fishing offers a five to ten second window where either you set the hook or you fumble through the motions. Beyond the obvious, prepare your mind and reflexes for the subtle bite.

Watch underwater footage of sport fish taking bait. Determine whether your quarry is a nibbler (walleye) or whether they inhale it with a gulp (northern pike). Contemplate these visuals while fishing and imagine that you know what you are missing. Estimate how many bites it would take to eat a night crawler and adjust your timing. Fish can pull the rod from your hand and they can steal your bait with a whisper. If you know what is normal, then you know when something is out of the ordinary (duh). Finicky fish require focus and readiness because they hit and spit. Get your head around the subtle bite and you will realize more fish and waste less bait.

Determine the disposition of what your fishing, adjust the presentation and the bite will change. Target solitary cruisers or ambush feeders that will give chase by trolling and casting. When fish strike a lure on the move, the bite will feel more definite, and that forward motion might cause the fish to hook itself. Inactive fish that are schooled up midday might do little more than open their mouths and slurp at a jig that is teased in their face. The intensity of a bite will also be affected by the amount of line in the water and the stretch of that line. Go braided if you are missing fish, and keep things close at hand. Slow your presentation when the action is slow, and concentrate on that reluctant bite.

Smaller fish can be more aggressive than the larger fish. Their bite can be like a machine gun, whereas the other is the bomb. Atop a school, alter your presentation if it seems you're catching that same small fish over and over. Big fish bite with the conviction that comes with practice and physical superiority. Post-chomp, they make that long hard pull until they feel resistance or taste something artificial. When you set the hook, big fish stay down and test the strength of your convictions. Lunkers enjoy more Super Big Gulps than your average gamer. Their bite might feel like a snag, until it moves.

Walleye are known for their soft and slow bite. With the right set-up, you can feel them chewing their way up that bait. When engaged, feed them line or drop your tip to minimize resistance. In the meantime, double-check to make sure your bail is locked and ready (not all reels have continuous anti-reverse). Soon those quiet nibbles become an obvious bite.

When jigging, bites are just as likely to come on a slack line fall. Watch the line to detect that it hasn't hit bottom. This can be a challenge when fishing chop and the boat is rocking. Light conditions make that 8 pound test line indistinguishable, so watch that depression in the water where the line enters. Anything that falls short or causes a stutter is bite. Keep the rod tip within your peripheral vision and glance to confirm that you've got a live one. The fish might be sitting still with the bait in its mouth. Slack line is the enemy. Stay in touch with the fish and maintain tension.

Northern pike may brush upside your bait or take several swipes before getting their mouth around it. The temptation is to stall or slow your retrieve to make it easier for the fish to take hold. Stay consistent and continue the action that attracted the fish in the first place. When working a spinner or buzz bait, note the amount of vibration during a normal retrieve, and be prepared for a fish to take the bait and keep that same pressure on the rod with only the vibration changing. If it be feeling like something ain't right and moving, set the hook. When casting for northerns in the shallow weed beds watch for bubbles or swirls behind your bait. Hold on for what follows.

Smallmouth bass behave with the same brash indignation as young fellers in sideways ball caps with flat brims and stickers. Like smallies, one gets on it and the others follow ready to jump in. When fishing with Buddy, if he has a fish on and under control watch behind the action and you might notice several more smallmouth following close behind. Keep a spare rod with a tube jig handy. You are after the elusive double-header and you may see the fish bite at your lure. Wait until you feel the fish before you set the hook.

Channel catfish get up in the bait to smell and taste with their barbels. With the boat on anchor, the scent trail sounds the chow bell, and the rod taps as they take it into their mouth and out. In heavy current, slack line is created when the rod is removed from the rod holder and if untouched, the bait might push a couple of feet away from the interested party. Compensate by reeling up those couple of feet as you release the rod from the holder. Working a bait-cast outfit, this might involve about five turns of the handle while being smooth and calculating. This effort requires coordination and patience that must supersede the excitement of the bite.

Stream fishing for rainbow trout requires the angler to find the pace of the drift and feel when it is interrupted. Use polarized sunglasses to identify impediments and flashes of fish turning. Shop the fly fishing department for small strike indicators that attach to your line. Unless you are hammering the hook jaws, the bite from a 'bow is less chomp and more clop.

Watching the line where it meets the water and if it finds resistance a wake will form behind it suggesting something fishy. Take breaks if you cannot maintain the concentration required to monitor the bite. Rainbow trout are easy to gut or gill hook with a live bait rig, so consider artificial lures when catch-and-release is the only option.

Not every fish will possess the bite of Mad Dog Vachon. Too much line out and you lose your touch; like talking through a tin can when the rope reaches down the block. Keep the fish closer and the signals become more pronounced. The hook set will be more immediate and powerful from the leverage gained when the fish are underneath the boat rather than way off to the side. Position the boat for short pitches, instead of long casts or trolling. The fish may be biting the same, but now you're feeling it.

Bobbers are not just for kids named Opie. Consider a scenario where the night before through circumstance you became desensitized and lost some capacity to function. Bobbers give your bait a straight up and down presentation and also go well with lawn chairs and cheeky drink cozies. Try casting a pick-erel rig with salted minnows from the dock. Over the years, I've caught bass, pike, perch, walleye, whitefish, and suckers all cruis-ing the same shallows out front the family cabin. Bobbers get everyone involved in the hysterics. Try different sized baits and hooks to find a combination that works in your area.

A challenging bite involves the fish swimming towards you with the lure in its mouth. This translates into a quick pull of the rod and then it springs up straight and the line goes slack. Bonus is that the fish is likely unaware of whatsup. Reel up that slack with speed and caution, anticipating a signal that the fish is still on. Don't reel up so fast that you pull the bait from the fish's mouth. Don't reel up so slow that the fish wises up.

Tired of being too fast with your hook set and coming up empty or being too slow and losing your bait? Remain calm and lift your rod until the line is tight and the tip begins to bend.

Watch your line for swimming movement. The fish doesn't want you to pull that bait away, but a little resistance might entice it to make quick work of it. Try not to second guess yourself or overanalyze your lack of success. Blame bad luck, Satan or Gary Bettman, but never your utter lack of experience.

Now Presenting

Your retrieve is an expression of your rhythm. There is the obvious: slow versus fast and consistent versus erratic approach. Reels with a low gear ratio are best for working it slow and deep. Reels with a high gear ratio can rip surface lures. Beyond equipment, how you present your lure is personal. Break from the norm, give a new look to pressured fish, and trigger that frenzy.

Start with an understanding what the lure is trying to mimic. Follow the manufacturer's instructions and your lure should run true. Experiment with different interpretations, but too much thinking defeats the purpose. Focus on the vibrations of the lure and how they are conveyed through line, rod and reel. If you have rhythm, you know when it is broken. That transition from reeling to hook set need be smooth. Anticipate the bite, but stay loose and don't get all sketched out. When in doubt, slow it down.

Chapter 4

Notes from the Outposts

How to be Eaten – Pt. 1

The Beaver floatplane returns in three days. The black bears return night and day. Deterrents should be the first line of defence, before you pull out the big guns. A greenhorn might question the hospitality of an outpost cabin with a spiked mat across the threshold and spiked mats under each window. Often it is a rectangle of three-quarter inch plywood into which a hundred or more nails are driven. This is not a meat tenderizer. These mats separate the men from the bears.

I've stayed in camps where the bears lurk nearby in the morning, conditioned to emerge to the sound of the boat motors leaving for a day of fishing. You cannot forget to put out the mats. The bears check every time. But remember after dark, not to wander too far to find relief. Those mats are just as effective on barefoot ogres with beer-filled bladders.

Use accordingly. Or party hard, crash and don't bother to put up the mats, dumbass. They are too heavy and pointy, you reason, between nips of schnapps. Sleep like Goldilocks, and meet a not-so-happy ending. Bears like fish, more than fishermen. But they also seem to enjoy variety, especially edibles that are fat and greasy.

If you ever have to kill a bear, use a high-powered rifle in at least .30 caliber, or a shotgun slug. You don't want to get any closer than you have to. You don't want to run out of ammunition before it is dead. Try for a broadside shot that targets the vitals that rest just behind the front shoulder. Bears look like humans when skinned. The meat is best in spring. Always bury a bear with its head facing north and do this without question.

The Story of the Trapper's Dog

There was something wolf-like against the rock outcrops, miles from civilization. I second-guessed myself but then witnessed his persistence. The trapper's dog survived the many months since spring and now seemed starved for, at the very least, attention. His act was half-wild, unsure of himself, yet knowing enough to chase the boat from island to island and to be here of all places at lunchtime. He shape-shifted between wild and tame.

The guide seemed put-off. The only person to blame was the trapper. There was no point in asking. The lodge owner could not allow a dog around camp. They were at capacity for mouths to feed and bodies in need of care. There were enough problems with bears, wolves, and staff. A pet would change the dynamic and force decisions that could otherwise be avoided. Yet here, for all to see, was this familiar friend free in the out of doors. It seemed inhumane.

My father cautioned me about wild animals but the dog was so pleased with the company that he forgot his killer instincts and dropped back into domestic life. The dog was all small and curious, dirty and skinny, skittish at first then joyous in performing some sort of four-legged jig. Maybe the trapper missed his backwoods companion – the dog that danced to his fiddle. I struggled to think the best of him. This was a good dog.

The guide let it slip, that this dog was spoiled because he only eats cooked fish. Maybe the guides watched over him. That dog ate like it was his last meal and I lavished him with attention. He ran the shoreline as the boat drove away. I liked to imagine that a guide took the trapper's dog home at season's end. Otherwise, I imagine he would not have lasted much longer out there all alone.

How to Commit Suicide by Mosquito

These things always happen during that last pass of the day. When the air turns cold and the sky turns denim. We were not too far from camp, but far enough that when the wind came up our boat was pushed back into a bay, out of sight out of mind. But we figured just one last pass because if you are going to catch a trophy fish, now's the time right?

We carry knives on our belts with distinction. It is the only requirement for dress. Yet on that night, we were shirtless and in our bathing suits. The whitecaps were pushing over the transom, so instead of back-trolling we faced the bow into the waves. We were somewhat protected from the wind, but the gusts pushed the boat to and fro at will, and then my drag was screaming. Before we realized what was happening, my reel was spooled and the boat motor conked. The propeller of the 9.9 horse kicker was seized in a tangle of my fishing line. We paddled for shore.

We had no tarp or blanket. It could be a long night under the boat. The cloud cover hastened the darkness as we reached shore. Here, I learned why my Father carries an Estwing hatchet. A knife could get the job done with time and light, we had neither. With clumsy precision he swung and the line exploded off the propeller like when you cut open an old golf ball. More tense moments. The motor didn't start on the first pull, for sure. And we never did finish that last pass, and so much for our trophies.

By the time we reached the main lake, it was dark and stormy and we were ill equipped. It took some time, but we followed the shoreline, somehow avoided the reefs, and arrived back at camp to the hoots and hollers of friends. They were just starting to get worried. Right. Never again.

How to Drown – Pt. 1

Sometimes there is no turning back. You've ventured to the far end of the lake and pissed away the day casting for pike in a weedy back bay. Sweet. No problems here, except that a shit storm is brewing out in the big lake. This is where the overnight bag comes in handy. Beach or anchor the boat and convert it to a camper by whatever means available. This is never your first choice, because of the worry a night in wilds may cause for loved ones. Better safe than sorry.

I remember crossing Gunisao Lake in a storm after an afternoon of fishing the rapids. To keep the boat from flipping from a rogue wave, I weighted the bow, tucked up against the burlap sack that held the fry pans. Our guide stood up to see what was coming and to get out of the spray. The boat banged with an intensity that would rival any Maiden concert. I expected the boat rivets to explode all at once like a dirty bomb. It was an uncomfortable hour. Our guide was experienced and we were never in real danger, but at the time, I appreciated the protection of a Floater jacket.

Human versus Animal

Were those the days? Brothers in arms with great stringers of fish strung between old-growth pillars or hung on rows of nails alongside the fishing shack. Hear the swoons of the burly men through curls of pipe smoke and the flap of oilcloth against wet flannel. Be in awe of the posse imposed over their kill, inflated chests and shit-eating grins, so proud and aloof. World domination implied with their display of casualties and for man alone! Eliminating the competition is human nature, yes?

It is wrong to characterize old people as mindless killers. (That's the video game generation). Over time we repeat this mistake and procrastinate away the slim chance of effecting change. At least back in the day, they had the courage to go out and get meat for dinner. Now, factory ships abetted by war technology use only boat hands to extract vast swaths of aquatic life. Others claim moral superiority while supporting monoculture and food factories that belch veggie dogs and soy cheese. It don't take Matlock to argue we remain guilty of abuse and neglect, and our recent disconnect with food production represents a step back. We have a sordid history of relations with the animals we eat. Appreciate the simple patience and understanding of freshwater fish, and stop making them out to be our enemies.

Whether you believe it or not, treat fish like they have feelings. And hell, why not assume they also enjoy a family life, blog following, a tawny port, and the benefits associated with several customer loyalty cards. (Ignore habits like eating their lovers and offspring). Be thoughtful and acknowledge when you are imposing. Act like a prick and coincidence will spit treble hooks in your direction. Fishing don't need George W. and the "either you are with us, or you are with the terrorists" bullshit mentality. Bodies of water are where hard-working folk find middle ground. Reflect on why we inject conflict into our relationships with nature and take pride in creating fear.

There are no opposing sides in fishing. People can imagine aspects of friendly competition, but the fish cannot. Perch are not against us. Goldeye are not out to get us. They ain't nothing but fish doing what they ought be. Yet like every living thing on this earth, they are fair game. No choice in the matter. Don't think

much of it, and it don't think much of me. Indifference should not be interpreted as rivalry though. Set out fishing with no preconceived notions of victory or defeat. Return knowing that fish and fisherman can coexist and go on to live to fight another day. You'll never know what you're missing if you stop fishing.

They had it right back when the packing for the long weekend fishing trip was a pound of butter and a change of underpants. Your tackle box was made of metal and held about a dozen well-used lures. You shaved with a hatchet, did most everything with whisky, and returned home after several days without contact. Shit happened for real, not through pics and quips in networks of anonymity. They lived more in the moment, and deserve the benefit of the doubt that their celebrated victories were over themselves and a hard upbringing, rather than the many fish.

Go looking for an enemy and the usual suspects will open you up to a new audience. Behave as if the cameras are rolling and the animal rights activists are circling. Refrain from outbursts or counter-protests that employ tactics like the bird, mooning, or bird/moon/rat combinations. Project an image of fishing that is mature and responsible. Accommodating others is not weakness. Practise empathy where bravado and ridicule are the norm. Document the beauty and tenacity of our fisheries or be threatened by outside interests that value moral beliefs or economy over culture.

Sport can function without winners and losers, because we are our own worst enemies. Participate, get your hands dirty, but do not antagonize. Respect the life that is interrupted by fishing. Fish are not in the water to serve our modern need for selfies. Give names to big fish and attribute to them human qualities, out of reverence for the ways they trick us into thinking they know better. If we've evolved in recent history, it is because we recognize the vulnerability of our fisheries and our right to fish. Today we celebrate that same mess of fish, by coming home with nothing to show for it but good friends. May future generations be impressed by our restraint.

How to Lose your Shit

In the dining area of the lodge, there stands a full-mount of a black bear, maybe six feet tall and broad at the shoulders. I'm not sure what he was served, but it appears to have disagreed with him. This boar is all claws and teeth. Perhaps, his presence is a reminder of the pecking order in remote locations.

Afraid of bears? Best keep that to yourself. It gets people talking about bears and most everybody opens with a terrifying story (nobody mentions their beloved teddy). Gets worse at night, when there are bears under the outpost cabin trying to determine which bed smells most of fear. Banging and scratching in a ghost-like fashion, come morning and the screen door's been torn and you can follow the path of destruction. Afraid of bears? Best keep that to yourself.

There are always crazy buggers at every lodge at any given time. They have ways of getting you punch drunk on beer, because then you have to piss in the middle of the night, real bad, and you stumble through the darkness waking everyone in the cabin in the process. And when you open the bathroom door that bear is standing before you, in your face and roaring. You won't have to take that piss (or shit) after all, and you'll pass out (again). Consider yourself warned.

This trick also works with a bear rug, but I advise caution. An angry drunk can summons the capacity for horrific violence. If he believes you to be a bear, be prepared to defend yourself. I know of a lodge that has a fine rug hung up on the wall just out of reach. At least one unfortunate soul felt an odd clawing at his face before he arose from his sleep. After the heart attack scare, the rug went up. Especially early in a trip, best keep your cards close to your chest because with little provocation, idle minds do the work of the devil.

How to be Eaten – Pt. 2

We set up camp on Culross Island near a stream turbid with chums and colour streaked with salmonberries. We ignored the well-worn paths littered with scat. The choice site was up safe from the North Pacific where the tidal range can push eighteen feet. It was probably also where the bears rested after their feasts. Whatever. Party animals have no known enemies! What could hurt us? Ourselves.

In a drunken stupor, we borrowed a 9mm semi-automatic handgun from a skipper from Newfoundland. As a Canadian citizen, my previous experience with this weapon was limited to the suction-dart and roll-cap versions. In an instant however, we had that blind confidence that only a gun can instill. Giddy almost.

We captained the dinghy, packing heat, and creeping on our rivals. We poured a little liquor on the shore to represent and for our crew back home in lock-up. To add to the act, we decided to play through some bear attack scenarios complete with the pow-pow effect. This is at about three in the morning. We were lucky that friendly fire didn't maim us both, thus enabling the bears to stretch their meal out for days. And we wouldn't have felt a thing.

We had a hard time finding the gun the next morning. Not cool. We later realized that the black bears in Prince William Sound are the size of poodles. Bears don't take kindly to surprises and we weren't looking to make friends. But in this case, offence is not a good defence. We made our bed and we should have lied in it. When you disrespect guns, they transform from a tool to a liability.

How to Lose Teeth

When amongst friends, certain laws governing international waters must be followed. A code of silence applies and infractions

are punishable by fist(s). The standard of proof is probable cause and the logic of drunken fools is permissible. No appeals.

This code of silence provides fellow enthusiasts with the confidence that no detail should be spared when sharing lurid tales of indiscretions with members of the opposite sex. Trust that together as anglers, we are free to live through others, to be as crass as our hosts allow, and yet remain polished in mixed company.

The bottom line should be obvious; after fishing don't go dishing to the better half. Spilling the beans = LTO.* And whoever invited you is now OTL.**

So, if you're one of those who don't get out much, who are big talkers when you get into the sauce, well say your peace and then shut up about it. We are here to fish, not to care about your stupid feelings. Best not to test them waters.

*   *Last Time Out*
** *On The List*

That being said, anglers are afforded a certain leeway when calculating the size of their catch, communicating the story of the fight, and anything else related to fishing. A general rule of thumb is that if your version of the events is 85 percent factual, then you are telling the truth. There is a sporting quality to making your story bigger, however all will suffer if certain standards are not upheld. Provide emphasis to entertain, but offend the intelligence of a dumbass, and you'll find your face broken.

How To Survive Family

Make yourself comfortable and know your place. Opening weekend is full of surprises and can be a stretch for camping up north of the Whiteshell. Yet every year it's a pilgrimage for uncles, brothers and cousins. In the high stakes world of family fishing trips, stories are formed here that will decide your place in history. This is a fitness test that don't involve no flexed arm hang, teddy-bear stands, or burpees. Recognize the cast of characters you are dealing with and realize you can't escape your family.

Make do with what you have. When shit goes down, more often than not, it happens on the far side of the lake. That hook became buried so deep into the tip of his thumb that it pushed into the bone. Some time later and back at camp, like the strongman game they assemble and attempt to muster the leverage to get the hook loose. No success. Call in the veterinarian. He uses a box cutter to expose more of the hook. Thankfully, it was still early in their trip and they had ample supply of their Irish family home remedy for pain relief. And after the vet was through, he gave him a nice pat of the head and a bandana to wear for the rest of the weekend. How's that for backcountry service!

Necessity is the mother of invention. After the thunderstorm incident, you learn to get the tarps up early. And as you learn (by way of physical and psychological abuse), you become driven to improve and practise one-upmanship. Do not rely on the rivets, you fool. Employ the golf ball method for securing the tarp. If one tarp is good, then ten tarps are impressive. Over the years, if you can see yourself through the torment and in-fighting your efforts might go unnoticed, and this is the ultimate compliment. The greater their faults, the better person you are for overcoming such an upbringing.

Specialized labour and complete reliance keep a family together. Every camp needs a firebug, tarp technician, cook/bartender, mechanic, medic, and jester. If you possess none of these skills, then you will find glory through fishing. Prove how much better you are than the lot of them through your command of beginner's luck. Don't expect the admiration that one receives by repurposing coat hangers into cup holders for the boat. There will always be next year, and your place is secure, because no matter how horrible of a boor you are, they can't shake you so easy.

Lake Trout on the Fire

· Head and gut the fish. Use your fingernail to remove all that bloody gunk that clings to the spine up and in the belly. Wash the fish and dry it inside and out.

· Coat the fish with oil and crust the skin with coarse sea salt, fresh ground pepper and some green herbs (rosemary, thyme, basil). Don't be stingy with the seasoning, as you want to infuse the fish with these flavours and the skin will be discarded.

· Stuff the fish with anything that resembles apples, lemons, onions, garlic, celery, and green pepper. Do not disrespect the fish with any store-bought stuffing or salad dressings. Just use salt and pepper and the microwave if you are that fucking stupid.

· Cook in a covered baking tin to contain the run off, or triple-wrap with tinfoil. Give it more of the indirect heat around the

fire and flip when half done. If need be, cut and wrap an individual portion that you cook as a tester.

· Take a butter knife and remove the skin. Do not remove the
gray fat as that makes the engine purr. Lift the meat from the
bones, add this and that from the stuffing, and use some bread
to mop up them fishy juices. If you are the best, add fiddle-
heads and mushrooms as sides, with raspberries and saskatoons for dessert.

· For lunch the next day, combine the leftover fish with herbed
mashed potatoes and form into patties. Add a panko crust, fry
in canola, and serve like burgers with all the fixings.

Chapter 5

Outfitted for Fishing

Kiss the Rod

Good fishing rods are made of graphite. You sure as hell don't want anything made of plastic, fiberglass, or metal. If you live in the suburbs and do all your shopping at big box stores, please proceed to the short pier for a long walk. Never buy a rod unless you have had it in your hands. Support local bait shops where their low-priced outfits are of good quality. Work your way through the rack and get a feel for the expensive though. Note the weight, balance and craftsmanship. Inspect the guides and female ferrule for nicks and imperfections. Compare rod tips and reel seats, as these often break. It is not uncommon for a rod to last ten years, so pay the extra for quality now because you can always trade up to a fancier reel in the future.

Consider the size of fish that you are pursuing and the style of presentation. Start with a spinning rod for ease of use and versatility. Labels on the rods will inform you of their composition and areas of specialty. Focus on the recommended line and lure

weights for the rod. Rough match the rod to your targeted quarry, and when in doubt, go lighter than expected. A lighter action set-up might cost you that trophy. But you won't be able to buy a bite with a heavier action set-up that fouls your presentation.

If you are up for the sport, try using an ultra-light for most everything. Big fish will bite small lures, but don't take this too far and overplay fish that you hope to release. Ultra-lights are manageable for kids and great for finesse work along shorelines and streams. Put the challenge and fun into catching trout, perch, goldeye, or panfish. Two-piece rods that are six feet or less will pack down nice for camping or hiking. Never buy a telescoping rod or some pocket-sized gimmick. These are for folk who cut their hair with the vacuum while alternating sets of ab blasting and ripe tomato cutting.

Start with a general purpose, medium-action rod that is six foot six inches in length. I prefer the sensitivity of a medium-light action rod when casting or jigging for walleye and bass. A medium-heavy action rod will have more backbone for long-line trolling. Shop different brands to find the middle ground that is right for your interests. One-piece rods have that direct connection from tip to handle. If I had to choose only one, it would be a six foot, medium-heavy spin rod that sells for less than $50.

If you're fishing early season in fast water where you have to toss a three-quarter-ounce bell sinker to keep the bait stationary, the matching rod needs enough substance to handle the current yet enough sensitivity to communicate the intentions of a fish that is tasting. This is the territory of seven feet or more in a medium-heavy to heavy action. When fishing for northern pike, muskie, carp, sturgeon, or channel catfish, you'll need the leverage to bring power to hook sets and horse them out of cover. Let's hope that you are catching so many large fish as to require a rod for that specific purpose.

Get Reel

What you don't want is a spin-cast reel. These are the sucky push-button variety that mount atop the rod, and bird's nest all the time and have horrific drag systems and hold very little line. Attach this waste of natural resources to a "fishing" rod endorsed by Hannah Montana and twerk your ass off the deep end, if that tickles your fancy.

Match your reel to rod, and this should reflect your choice of line and lure weight. If I had to choose only one reel, it would be a medium-sized spinning reel with a ten ball bearings system for under $50. Other features to consider when purchasing a fishing reel:

1. The gear ratio refers to how many times the spool turns with each turn of the reel. Lower gear ratios generate more torque for a slow, deep retrieve. Higher gear ratio means more speed for working spoons and surface baits. A bait-cast reel with a 5.1.1 gear ratio, gives you the torque to work the deep stuff without having to use so much raw power. Big fish chase big lures, and big lures create all sorts of drag. A spinning reel with a 7.1.1 gear ratio, gives you the ripping speed for working spoons and surface baits. When casting, that speed also helps to take up line from a fish that took your lure and is swimming towards the boat.

2. Drag systems can be judged by the smoothness of operation and the ease of adjustability. You want a sealed unit to protect from the elements, and it's nice to have visual and audible references for when you adjust the drag. A continuous anti-reverse system will ensure your hook sets are solid and your drag engages at any point during your retrieve.

3. The number of ball bearings in a reel is directly correlated to the retail price. Turn the handle and feel how she rolls. Like the hit song, you want a smooth operator. A reel that has at least a four-bearing system is recommended.

4. The lighter the reel the better, but not at the expense of durability. An aluminum reel body or spool is good, but you don't want lightweight through cheap plastic parts.

5. Ergonomics and design features help lay the groundwork for a long-term relationship. Slide your fingers between the reel post and grip the reel foot to determine how well it fits your hand. Extras include a trigger to flip the bail and line keepers on the spool.

One Toke Over the Line Sweet Jesus

Shop for a quality fishing line like you shop for condoms. The spec list calls for material that is thin and sensitive, yet strong and durable. Unique applications require more protection from friction, abrasion, and such. Under muddy conditions, for instance, you might require high visibility neon. Perhaps a lighter touch for tight spots, or something heavy if yours is too quick of a response to the slightest tug. Treat the line like an extension of yourself. If you're new to fishing, for a time you may be happy just wetting a line, but for that feeling to endure, consider the following rules of thumb:

1. Don't buy old stock – avoid dollar stores and garage sales
2. Don't trust damaged goods – remove any questionable sections
3. Proper storage is a must – do not jeopardize the integrity of the product

But above all else, ignore the marketing. First and maybe only thing you need to know is that you will fork over ten bucks for 330 yards of monofilament or twenty-five bucks for 150 yards of braid. End of conversation? The manufacturers will describe how they've fused titanium and diamond thread with the pubic hair of dominant silverback gorillas to create an invisible line that also serves as anchor rope and dissolvable stitches.

Moreover, they suggest you change your line two or three times a season, plus on Father's Day, Christmas, and your birthday. It matters how serious you take your fishing. As far as I can remember, I change my monofilament in the spring of each year. Though there may have been some lost years...

Quality fishing line is a function of strength versus diameter. Smaller diameter line is less visible to fish. Smaller diameter line offers less resistance in the water, so crankbaits can dive deeper. A reel holds more smaller diameter line that large diameter line, and that extra twenty or thirty yards can be the different between landing and losing a trophy fish.

Other factors in choosing a line include resistance to abrasion, stretch, and manageability. Fishing factors include water clarity, fish activity, lure choice, and presentation. Decide for yourself through trial-and-error, but here's my take on monofilament versus fluorocarbon versus braided:

Monofilament

1. Manageable – easy to cut, tie, and untangle
2. Stretches – forgiveness to over-anxious anglers, action for top-water baits
3. Floats — for use with surface lures and shallow crank baits

Fluorocarbon

1. Invisible – important in clear water on sunny days with finicky fish
2. No stretch – for solid hook sets in tough cover
3. Sinks – for use with jigs and deep-diving crank baits

Braided Line

1. Super Strong – for flipping, pitching, and nasty cover
2. No Stretch – better sensitivity for trolling through cover like weed beds
3. No Memory – manageable and smooth casting

Braided line requires more attention to spooling your reel and tying knots. Braid is so strong that you might break your rod or reel on a snag if you are not careful, especially when trolling. Braid is more conspicuous, but this can be mitigated by tying a double uni knot to attach a fluorocarbon leader to the last section of line before the lure. Keep your leader to around six feet in length, or a bit less than the length of your rod. That gives you room to flip or pitch without the joining knot getting caught up in you rod guides. This hybrid approach can be more time consuming to rig, but is becoming the gold standard.

I don't use braid are because I am a creature of habit who is also cheap and lazy. Most important, I think a line should be easy to cut and re-tie. Checking for nicks and abrasions should be part of your routine each time you change lures. I usually run the last four feet of line through my lips to sense the imperfections. If a line is easy to cut and re-tie, you won't think twice about removing the damaged section. Take care of this detail and you will break off fewer fish.

When storing your fishing rod, never place the hook in the rod guides and tighten up your line. This is a great way to break your rod tip and to create nicks in your guides. Over time, as your line travels the surface of your guide, those nicks will damage your line. Most rods have a hook keeper near the handle for this purpose.

I also question the wisdom of allowing your gear to bake in the rod lockers of your boat all summer. Or in the off-season storing your lines outside and subjecting them to freeze and thaw cycles. I have no facts or research to support an opinion that extremes in temperature affect the performance of fishing line. I got thinking this way from fly fishing, where top-quality lines can set you back a c-note. Fishing is about the detail, and line is a good place to be obsessive.

Being from Winnipeg, I can't help but dispense advice on being thrifty. That first fifty yards of line on the spool is backer that only sees the light of day if you hook a lunker or the boat propeller. That last fifty yards of line gets the most wear and tear. To get an extra year out of your line, turn it ass-backwards. Mark the end with a piece of tape, strip all the line from the spool, and retie the taped end to the spool. This works even more awesome if you want to transfer the line to another rod.

Line choice also reflects your sporting nature. You may be able to coax a small fish into biting on heavy tackle, but that's a catching mentality. Small fish can be big fun if you are a fair match with lighter line and tackle. Consider the weight of a trophy of the species that you are targeting. Choose a reel that is designed to perform best with a comparable line weight. Get a rod that balances with the reel and use lures within the range of weights specified on the rod.

- 4 pound test – trout, perch, crappies, goldeye
- 8 pound test – walleye and bass
- 20 pound test – northern pike, lake trout
- 30 pound test – channel catfish, muskie

If you get in a tangle, take special care when disposing of old line. Fixing for a smack upside the head if you litter the shore. Line creates a nasty snare for mink, muskrats, and beaver. It tends to constrict as they struggle, resulting in loss of limb, starvation, or easy pickings for a predator. Take care, even if you are placing line direct into the garbage. It can get tangled up with the Canada geese and bald eagles that loiter around the landfill. Be a patriot.

Wrap all the old line around your hand to create a loop. Take your knife and cut opposing ends of the loop making small pieces of line. Put it in the trash or in the disposal units available in tackle shops and at popular fishing spots. That good will come back to you sooner or later.

Spooling the Reel

Check your reel for the manufacturer's recommendations for line weight and yardage. For once, do as you are told. Start by tying a basic knot close to the tag end. Bring the line through the guides of the rod. Open the bail, tie two overhand knots (the double uni), and pull tight to the spool. The knot on the tag end should pull tight to the double uni. Close clip the tag end and find a friend.

When braided line slips on the spool, the reel can turn and turn with no line retrieved. First put masking tape around the spool to give the braid something to grip. Or tie on a mono-filament backer that is long enough to cover the spool. Use a comparable pound-test to the braided in case a big one takes you to the end of your rope.

Avoid twists by orientating the plastic spool of line on the vertical so that the line falls from the spool the same way it was placed on there by the manufacturer. Have your friend hold the line, using a pen or pencil through the centre of the spool to allow it to freewheel. Use your two fingers near the lead guide to apply consistent pressure to line while reeling. Do not fill the entire spool or the memory of the line with cause it to overspill. Leave about one-quarter of an inch vacant on spinning reels.

This process can be made easier with automatic line spoolers with adjustable tension, yardage counters, and craft beer on tap (some modifications necessary). Quick line changes make it possible to use one reel for a variety of species and fishing conditions. And that my friend is how you justify buying an auto spooler and Shimano Stella reel. In the old days, you could also buy extra spools for your reel that you could preload with different lines for quick changes. Fly fishers seem to be the only ones smart enough to keep that going.

Tie Yourself in Knots

To practice, get a length of wool from the cat or turn your leather sweater to a vest already. Learn a fishing knot that you can tie fast and consistent with the lightest of lines. And tie that knot over and over and over. Tie it with gloves on, tie it in the dark, tie it when your hands are frozen and your mind unsound. Slip up and yikes! That's why you do not "invent" your own fishing knot. Follow instructions for once, and save the creativity for your crocheting and scrapbooking. Learn to adapt, experiment, and take these suggestions:

- Inspect the line for any damage before tying on a lure. Run it through your fingers or lips and remove any offending sections.
- I fish monofilament line and use the Trilene knot. When tying any knot with monofilament, always lubricate the line with spit, so the knot pulls tight without generating heat.
- Braided lines are slippery, which may cause your standard knot to pull free at a most inopportune moment. When fishing jigs or single hook lures, use the Palomar knot. For convenience, use the Berkley knot when fishing larger lures with a mess of treble hooks.
- Don't forget to tie the tag knot when securing your line to the spool with a double hitch.
- The double-uni knot is used for connecting lines, including the monofilament to braided connection. Remember, any knot with all them turns requires great gobs of gob.
- Tie the Rapala knot for crank baits because it creates a loop that allows the lure a little more play versus the direct knot. This should improve the action and reduce line twisting.

Out of necessity, a swivel, snap and/or leader often interrupts the direct connection between line and lure. Take a look at what saltwater anglers are using to get a perspective of what little things come into play at their scale. Seek out freshwater gear that incorporates the same welded split rings and ball bearing swivels. Snaps should be shaped to reduce resistance and maximize action. Look for designs that use only one piece of wire that twists back and locks onto itself. Keep a variety of sizes on hand to go as small as possible without creating a weak link. A direct connection is always best, but otherwise take these suggestions:

- Leaders can be used for deceptive purposes by going clear and thin for the last two feet before the lure. Fish a stocked trout

pond with those tiny hooks attached to ultra-light lines with factory snell knots.

- Steel leaders that are eighteen inches in length are a must when fishing for toothy fellers like the northern pike. Use at least the twenty-pound test variety and look for supple construction so not to impede the lure action.

- A snap and swivel adds convenience for when fishing with kids. Give them a mini pair of needle nose pliers to open the clasp, and the independence to change their own lures and experiment at will.

- The swivel alone helps avoid line twist when trolling a big in-line spinner buck tail. Any other scenario and the risk of the swivel failing or getting caught up in a rock is not worth the small benefit.

- Three-way swivels are used for bottom-bouncer rigs when trolling or in current. Floating or unweighted hooks offer little resistance when working live baits, while the weight and not the hook, gets sacrificed in a snag situation.

· When jigging or casting for bass and walleye tie direct because the slower presentation allows a closer inspection. Only change to a swivel, snap, and/or leader for convenience, if you are breaking off fish, or having your line foul from twist.

That Sinking Feeling

When it's time to get down on it, check the specs on your rod and reel, and follow the range of lure weights that they recommend. Duh, I've said that before. I know, but when will it sink in? For environmental reasons, consider using weights that are not made of lead, especially on lakes or in areas that have high fishing pressure. What is the lake without the call of a loon at dusk? However minute the chance, I want no part of creating that silence. And anglers should get out front of this one, before we are cast as the murders of waterfowl. Force the government to get involved and we'll be at the mercy of the retailers and manufacturers (they have no mercy). Yet really, how much more will it cost to keep lead out of fishing? If you are losing that many weights for it to make a difference, than you need to reconsider whether you have the skill set to participate in the first place. Before we get too heavy, weigh these options:

· *Split shot* – use in current for trout and with bobbers and live bait. Buy the type that can be opened and closed, and fine tune the weight so that your bobber will fall below the surface with a slightest pull.

· *Bell sinkers* – use with pickerel rigs when fishing the rivers in your city. Don't buy the pyramidal sinkers as they snag and get so stuck in the muck as to diminish the force of your hook set (and I'm sure that force is considerable, so beware).

- *Rubber-core* – add to an existing rig to avoid retying, and you will be punished for being lazy. The rubber untwists when fighting a fish and you will be left with a small and empty zipper bag. And we all know where that gateway leads.

- *Worm weight* – painted up and a rattle added, these in-line weights makes for a fine bassin' rig of the weedless variety. Or add rubber stops and beads to replace shot and the nicks or crimps they leave in your line.

- *Dragging weights* – used in Lindy rigs or fashion together with a three-way swivel for trolling your bait at a set distance from bottom. Get inventive and use to target suspended fish with the same ideas behind a downrigger.

- *Bottom bouncers* – use for walleye that are off a rocky bottom. Weights get snagged just like hooks, and the wire feeler keeps you connected to bottom without risking a round, bulky weight. Can also be used to weight a floating plug and run it deep.

Get Your Hooks Into It

Begin your lesson with a trip to the museum to see how the Inuit and First Nations people got it done with style. Prized carvings of ivory and bone are now manufactured from wire and coated for sharpness, strength and longevity. There is no functional standard for hook sizing and perhaps no need for the obvious. Lures are sold with hooks, and together they should run true to create a distinct action. Unless you are fishing with kids and want to replace trebles with singles, leave good enough alone. A better understanding of the parts of hooks will help more in fishing live bait rigs:

- *Eye* – should be closed for strength, positioned straight, large enough that can you thread your line without the use of a microscope.
- *Shank* – longer lengths allow more control when fishing plastics and crawlers. Can be bent and turned to weed less, barbed to hold bait, or shaped to a fly-tiers specifications.
- *Bend, Throat, and Gap* – these are parts of a hook and that's all you need to know.
- *Barb* – required only by those who need every advantage to land a fish.
- *Point* – edged like a spear, needle, knife or some deadly combination of running with scissors and a poke in the eye with a sharp stick.

Check the hook for sharpness and shape after any snag. Once these attributes become a given, make small adjustments to solve nagging problems. For instance, I use needle nose pliers to give a slight, right offset to the hooks on jigs. Might be superstition, but I believe I land more walleye than without. When using a crawler harness, I choose hooks with large eyes. Feed the bait over the eye, pass a toothpick through the bait and eye and bait, and then break off the toothpick flush. This will hold your bait in place, disguise the hook, and force the fish to take it all in their mouth. So whether it's jimmying rig a rubber band to create a weed guard or using a segment of plastic worm to hold your minnow on the hook, fishing rewards nuance and refinement.

Bait & Switch

I can't begin to explain all the shit out there. Many lures catch only suckers. Start with some rigs and weights, an assortment of jigs and tails, couple of spoons, couple of plugs, couple of spinners, and a surface bait. That's it. Get the smallest tackle box you can find. Resist buying a larger tackle box until you demonstrate proficiency with what you have. I respect an angler with the confidence to travel light and the versatility to adjust their presentation instead of changing lures. The variety of lures available for purchase is ridiculous. End of discussion. There is much more to fishing than another shiny thing you can buy at the store on impulse.

I think ROY G BIV is my only memory of high school science (and the chorus to Thomas Dolby's "Blinded by Science"). If ROY G BIV were still teaching today, he'd promote the use of bright lures during bright light conditions. That would be ROY talking about the red, orange and yellow end of the spectrum. BIV would speak out for darker lures during low light conditions (and the return of New Jack Swing). In neutral conditions, choose a silver or white. That being said, my favourite jig combinations are the pink head and white tail, and the orange head and chartreuse tail. I prefer silver to gold spoons, and I really like the blue and silver combination because I think it looks like a cisco (the baitfish, not the singer of "The Thong Song").

JT's Top 10 Classic Lures

1. Len Thompson Spoon – ¾ ounce in five of diamonds
2. Mepps Syclops Spoon – 1 ounce in silver chartreuse
3. Mepps Agila Spinner – ¼ ounce in gold
4. Spinnerbait – ½ ounce, chartreuse skirt, double willow blades in hammered steel
5. Berkley Power Tubes – 3" size in pumpkin seed
6. Canadian Wiggler – in firetiger pattern
7. Rapala Shad Rap – 3/8 ounce in bleeding perch pattern
8. Rapala Ripping Rap – ½ ounce in red crawdad

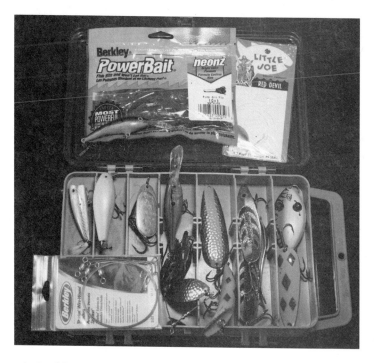

9. Berkley Walleye Rig – spinner in hammered silver
10. Suick Jerk Bait – 9" in sucker pattern
11. The Red & White – with or without beady eyes, this spoon is Canadian

Common Scents

Fish can smell. Not like fishy, but like they have the sense (without the nose for it). If you're filling with jerry cans or changing tanks over, being careless results in gas in the bottom of the boat that sloshes over everything. Same if you lather yourself with aftershave, sunscreen or bug dope and handle your line or lures with too much touchy-feely. What's wrong with you? The fish won't stop to smell your roses. At minimum, the lure should be unscented.

I've heard of guys using WD-40 on their lures as an attractant. Same guys use duct tape to make back pockets on their sweatpants. (Scary what that attracts). And you don't want to know what they do with penetrating oil. Anyhoo, the popular chemical spray does create a rainbow sheen in the water that resembles the scales and salt effect of frozen minnows. But don't be foolish; it's really just pollution.

Most everyone works jobs they hate in order to vacation in Mexico and act like assholes for a week each year. Now allow these fools to be your mules. While enjoying winter, ask them to risk their matching ponchos and return bearing two bottles of pure vanilla extract. Use one bottle when baking and to flavour yogurt. Add a spray pump to the second bottle and use as fish attractant. It may not make any difference, but on a slow day you want to feel like you're doing everything you can. Or you can buy plastic baits that are impregnated with the fish version of high-fructose corn syrup and meth. These additives may provide an edge, but if that fishy smelling concoction spills, it will haunt you.

Chapter 6

From the Depths of Civilization

The Urbane Angler

A ragtag group once claimed to have built a city on rock 'n' roll, and many have repeated their chorus since. I believe this possible, if this city was also built around a body of water that holds fish. Fish can sustain a population, and when in abundance, create opportunity for trade. Rock 'n' roll facilitates procreation, circle of life, and so concludes my lesson on the industrial revolution. Moving along.

When fishing, you become familiar with the character of a city. In Winnipeg, we are river folk of the Red, Assiniboine, Seine, and La Salle. What is hip and cosmopolitan about fishing is the gathering of old-timers, local heroes, trophy takers and armchair anglers. Your paths may never cross otherwise.

As John Fogerty sings, "people on the river are happy to give". They may give you hell for casting over their line, and they are just as quick to give you unsolicited advice. And then there are the crazies that stop to talk fishing. All walks of life lead to water at some point, and here in the mix you discover that you belong amongst such eccentrics. The river runs through us (especially if you dare take a drink). The people on the river are happy to give you the courage to leave the house in sweatpants, and spend the day reclined on the shoreline and picking potato chips out of your chest hair, worm guts out of your finger nails. Winnipeg is a fishing theme-park.

Imagine these urban bodies of water also holding man-eating monsters and hideous mutants sparked by toxic waste. Though I have failed to meet said oddities face-to-face after many years spent trying, if you fish, these creatures are of interest because of the secrets they could reveal about the depths. And if you consume their flesh, you will gain superpowers.

We fear what it all about, until we discover the beauty it holds. These are the waters that you pass over each day during the commute. Keep a fishing rod in the trunk and listen to those urges.

Star Attractions

Parks and green spaces offer free access to fishing spots, with the added bonus of nearby garbage and washroom facilities. Our soulless modern suburbs are often void of this square footage, as the one percent occupy the waterfront with their monuments to insecurity. Respect property owners and empathize with their aversion to hobo fires, but consider using rights-of-way for utilities or flood pumping stations to reach that shoreline. Learn your spot. Fan-cast the area to pinpoint the snags, and as levels and current vary throughout the season, go short and long to work the slow and fast waters. Use these urban entry points to launch float tubes, canoes, and kayaks. Exercise our right to access and navigate these waters.

Shit goes down under a bridge. This is a crime scene for chronic litterbugs and looters, so prepare to capture all likes of mattresses, shopping carts, zombies, BMX bikes, and artificial Christmas trees. These treasures are also structure for fish. Avoid the snags aplenty by fishing just downstream and try to tuck your lure into the slack water eddies. Careful of how you fish around the support structures of the bridge, because you don't need your line to abrade on the concrete. In this junkyard, bring your heavy gear and be ready for all sorts of finagling.

Factory or city works are good targets for the catch-and-release anglers out for fun. Old cities still often rely on combined sewer systems to move shit around. When that large storm hits and the pipes become overwhelmed, "relief" is provided by dumping the untreated flow into the nearest body of water. From a fish perspective, these warmer waters are nutrient-rich, feeding aquatic vegetation to create cover and attract minnows and other food sources. From a human perspective, this pollution is unacceptable and we should lobby government to fund infrastructure improvements. In these parts, trophy fish include the three-eyed Blinky and those Jesus fish that are immortalized on car bumpers. (Don't eat the Jesus fish. It tastes like chicken.)

Tackle Anything

In Winnipeg, I access the Red River where it meets St. Vital Park. From our spot on the outside bank of a sharp turn, we cast into fifteen feet of water at the most. Pickerel rigs keep it simple. For a dollar or so, the rig deploys two single hooks that are suspended near bottom. There be magic in this particular combination of swivel, beads, wire arms, snap, and sinker. I prefer my rigs strung with twenty-pound test monofilament, #2 hooks with long shanks, and a ¾ ounce bell sinker. Adjust the rig to current (more weight) and quarry (smaller hook).

Use rod holders to keep your hands free for skipping rocks, propping up your head, and general scratching purposes. In the bushes, we stash sticks with a fork at one end and a point at the other. The fork holds the rod upright and the point anchors in the mud, stupid. Careful not to poke yourself in the eye. And if I ever catch you throwing those sticks in the river, it's sink or swim for you. The stick should be about three feet total, leaving a couple of feet protruding from the mud when secured.

Another approach is to use a three-foot length of 2" ABS pipe. At one end, use a hacksaw to cut an angle or point for driving the pipe into the earth. Place a two-by-four block on the top before striking with a hammer. If you want to get all fancy, cut a three-quarter inch notch in the pipe that allows your spinning reel to drop further and thereby locks your rod in the desired position.

Competition can be found in casting. There remains that challenge to hit the far bank regardless of how impossible that may prove over the years. Henceforth, when going to great lengths choose a longer rod of the medium-heavy variety. I like two-piece rods because they are easier to carry when riding your bike. Practise your overhead power cast with generous amounts of body English.

Chances are you own a hip pack and that you remain perplexed why they fell out of fashion. From that soft leatherette to the many zippers, you found nothing more svelte for holding smokes, a Zippo, and a hacky sack. If you are of a younger generation, you already carry a man purse so no matter. Remove the scented stationary and emery boards, and pack extra rigs, pliers, and a knife. You need to be self-contained and self-sufficient, so not to lose your spot on the bank. For when you catch that big fish, prepare for other anglers to emerge from the bushes and begin crowding you out. They don't fear bulging hip packs or respond to the cold shoulder, so best establish barriers to entry before the inevitable happens.

I use nightcrawlers and only nightcrawlers. I target fish of all types and sizes, not just the big uns. I know a spot down the old dike road where folks have dumped their leaves and lawn waste for years. Peel back some of them composting layers with a pitchfork, dig underneath, and break up them clods to find real "juicers". Use your thumbnail like a cutting wheel to piece the worm and bait both hooks of a pickerel rig. Feed the worm up the shaft of the hook and only leave an inch or so hanging loose.

Frozen bait works dandy, as smell is more important than movement. Minnows, shrimp, squid, and frogs all bring the funk. Larger baits are a mouthful and attract fewer strikes but more trophies. Your responsibility when bait fishing is to be attentive and risk losing fish to early hook sets versus waiting too long and getting the gut. Bring the intensity. You don't have to always watch your rod tip, but it needs to be in your sphere. Sunflower seeds help maintain focus and create a sense of rhythm. Feel all things riparian and build sensitivity to abrupt change. Or just get a bell off your Christmas sweater and try not to snore.

Combat Fishing

The title of this section is inappropriate. It implies warfare, and although this style of fishing requires a certain indifference to other anglers, it does not involve winning at all costs. No fish is worth a whip from the pistol grip of a bait-cast rod. There are no enemies in fishing.

When fishing for reds on the Russian River, ignore the guy with the .357 Magnum lashed to his side. He'll be the first one to be mauled when the bear arrives to the party. Unlike others, do not ignore the woman caught up in the river. Stop fishing and grab her from the fast moving water. Share pleasantries, but in no way are you obligated to share your spot on the river. In Alaska, it's as much about protein in the freezer for the family and jars of smoked salmon to send home with friends from the lower 48. These fisheries lend themselves to a catching mentality and therein lies the problem with combat fishing.

There will always be popular spots like wading under the locks at Lockport. Enjoy the camaraderie and antics, or fish at night. Get some glow sticks and pass time raving for all I care. Watch them sparks from the shore fire intermingle with the stars, and hear all them critters that are talked over and shooed off. Pick your battles, and get back to fishing where you can feel the loneliness and tranquility of our nature. Fishing seems dangerous at night. Sleep when you're dead.

How to Drown – Pt. 2

Combat fishing is about positioning, and it's dang near impossible to help yourself from getting out there in the depths. I've been drawn into such Man Competitions,* from Ship's Creek to the Red River, and it brings a rush of excitement. Where does the drop-off start?

Think about all that silt you're stirring up, the sound of your knees knocking in the current, and the shadow you cast over the stream. Many of you are sturdy individuals with enough substance to change the flow rate of most creeks, streams and small rivers. Damn straight!

What are your actions telling the fish about you? Friend, you are a menace. You're out stomping on fish habitat. In spring, fish are on their nests in the shallows. And I've caught lots of fish within ten feet of the shoreline.

But you're in the zone, right? The faster water where any sort of debris floating downstream will hit you high (hopefully right upside the head), then you'll topple and probably take a couple others with you. You need a knife to cut them waders free but that can be hard to find amongst all those gadgets that took your breath away in the store. That extra bulk now adds to your tangle. Quick, empty your pockets for a second time.

*   *Winner proves his ignorance and loser gets hurt in the process*

A better start would be with some real boots. Save your tri-colour Chuck Taylor's for the high school reunion. Rocks are made slippery, especially in places that are fit for Man Competitions. Consider boots with felt, studs, or sticky rubber bottoms.

Lose the clown pants by securing a belt over top your waders. That belt will keep water from pouring in. Better yet, buy waders made from neoprene or some super-fabric that is resistant to rips and abrasions. New waders are lighter and can also help keep you cool or warm when standing in a stream all day. Consider a pair that will also work for waterfowl hunting.

I recognize that this well-intentioned advice may be falling on deaf ears. After drowning your sorrows, you feel that fishing is the only place for you. That's fine and dandy, I understand that you are of the mesh tank, jam shorts and barefoot variety. I suggest you get a length of rope and tie your stupid self to a tree so as you don't end up at the bottom of shit's creek. There be enough snags there already.

Trash versus Trophy

Silver carp are known in North America as that twenty-pound alien that jumps ten feet from the water to exact terror upon the groin of an overweight man in undersized overalls. He pilots a boat made of pallets, powered by alcohol, and the silver carp seem aware, organized and determined. It's hard not to like these fish, but government men named Eugene or Cornie will try to convince you that silver carp are invasive. These skittish fellers jump in response to the vibration of a boat motor, and their habits of consumption and reproduction bruise the egos of our native fish. They are not welcome.

We have a habit of marginalizing new immigrants through name-calling, but trust the restaurant lobby to fund PR campaigns for the "silverfin". I would argue that the common sucker also needs rebranding. Or maybe we just need to start thinking for ourselves. Hungry people dream of fish that jump into the boat. Maybe we are due for a trim, or maybe we choose to get over the mindset that we are better than everyone else. A wild fish sounds more appetizing than a 'farm' fish fed a diet of industrial waste. Call it what you want, but we will have to eat away at the problems associated with silver carp. Now, can we manage without resorting to name-calling?

(Full disclosure: I am in the preliminary stages of securing investment for a silver carp juice marketed as a beverage additive to enthusiasts of krunk music.)

One of my favourite pursuits is to cast for northern pike in shallow weed beds. There's no mistaking their bite and fight, and as table fare, they are among the best. The northern pike is also a most impressive trophy. They look prehistoric-strong and can be posed to appear rather perturbed. Yet in spite of their majesty, the northern pike has a mixed reputation.

Most guides favour walleye to pike, because pike lures often have multiple treble hooks and clients have multiple casting issues. Also, the Y-bones along the back of a pike can challenge the average filleter. And despite their larger size, too many people mistake pike flesh as inferior to walleye. Immature fish are called snakes or hammer handles. In Alaska, I learned that northern pike are an invasive species, because horror of horrors, they eat young salmon.

Outdoor enthusiasts need be careful with our tone and the way we speak amongst ourselves. What starts as good intentions can wreak havoc for future generations. It ain't right to be cruel to animals. And if you don't have something nice to say, shut the hell up. We may think we've found good reason to favour one species or another, but lord have mercy, we sure don't have a great track record. Moreover, this divisive rhetoric takes the

fun out of fishing by giving young people the wrong impression of what constitutes a trophy.

When I was young and even more stupid, we had this spot in the city where we'd catch rock bass and sauger. (Funny thing, this fishing hole also produced the odd northern pike. Here, a juvenile pike was the prize fish. Go figure.) Problem being was that for every "good fish" that we would catch, we would also hook several bullhead. And we would take pleasure in killing the bullheads, because we could and because we reasoned that it would improve our chances of catching better fish. We'd toss bullheads over our shoulder and up the bank, and they would use their pectoral fin spines to shimmy their way back into the water. How could we disrespect a fish with such tenacity?

The first fish that my son and daughter caught was a bull-head. Their exotic look only helped secure interest in a way of life that involves catching and eating fish. If a bullhead is what I catch first, imagine what is to come. Some fear an invasion and fight to win at all costs, while others see an opportunity to engage more anglers or rally widespread support for fisheries conservation. The Manitoba Master Angler program awards a diamond badge as the highest level of achievement for anglers who register one trophy fish in twenty different species. Each one of these trophies is of equal value, and that's a sportsman's approach to fishing.

Thou shall not get caught up on appearances, because we are ugly folk. Sure, rainbow trout are so well packaged that you wanna peel back their skin and eat them like an ice cream sandwich. You may not think the same of a bullhead. But as you incorporate fish into your diet you will find a place for both exotic and utility fare. Trash or trophy, it's what fuels a love of the outdoors.

Baba Lee Rodrigue's Petersfield Patties

· Start with two pounds of Netley Creek's finest, be it sheepshead, white bass, and/or catfish. If you're up in the winter, northern pike do up nice. Perform the basic fillet and skin.

There's no need to remove pin bones as these will get ground and fried to oblivion.

· Griswold's #2 cast iron meat grinder is one of many classics for the countertop. I highlight this model because the Griswold's were also known for the discerning style and function of their wood-paneled station wagon. Get the *Vacation*-feel while working them raw fillets through the fine ground plate and into a mixing bowl.

· Add breadcrumbs, an egg, and spice with Lawry's Seasoning Salt and dried parsley. Deviate from the recipe and you must call it by another name. Mix the fish and such, form patties, and let sit in the refrigerator for an hour or so to set.

· Cover the patties with an egg wash and coat with breadcrumbs. Hit those patties hot and fast will lard or vegetable oil in a fry pan. The burger bun should be toasted and buttered. Accessorize with burger fixings or a homemade tartar sauce. And make extra patties to eat on the way to the dock, early the next morning.

Chapter 7

How to Catch More Fish

Fish On!

A general rule of thumb: your hook is sharp when it can scratch the top of your nail. I choose to etch the logo for Twisted Sister into the nail of my middle finger. Decide for yourself. Check for sharpness when you tie-on. Snags can bend and dull your hooks. A few well-placed strokes of a hand file will smooth the rough edges. You need the point of the hook to penetrate past the barb, and that involves piercing bone and cartilage.

Use a long sweeping motion to set the hook. Start low and pull up hard. This is a power move that should originate in your core. Two hands are better than one. A longer rod provides more leverage and often has an extended butt section that serves as an anchor point. A shorter rod is faster and easier to maneuver when fishing wooded shorelines. Better too hard a hook set, than too soft.

When you feel that resistance, freeze for a moment. Prepare to absorb an explosion of energy. There is a tendency to relax the tension on the line and drop the rod tip before bearing down and reeling. Avoid that, especially when fishing with barbless hooks.

If you are fishing with live bait, choose a generous portion. It may seem like you are chumming the waters and emptying your wallet, but the extra time this affords will help you get a feel for the action. Consider adding a stinger hook.

Have a basic understanding of the mouth of your quarry and their tendency to bite. You might be faster to avoid the gut hook. Even worse are foul-hooked fish because they make you believe you've caught a beast like no other. A fish hooked in the body creates formidable resistance when dragged sideways through the water. A fish hooked in the tail will cause you rod tip to thump like mad and pull drag at will. Avoid disappointment by being at the ready.

You Gotta Fight for Your Right to Party

Bring a fair fight and assess the situation before you act on it. Don't delay in getting a basic understanding of what's on the end of the line and how well you are equipped. The fish may be giving you the headshake or bulldogging it down deep. Don't just start haulin' ass because this ain't no tractor pull. There is no dignity in forcing a fish to waterski up to the boat. Squirrels and chipmunks have owned that act ever since *That's Incredible!*.

Keep your rod tip above your waist and always pointing upward. Reel as you lower your rod from a 1 o'clock position to a 3 o'clock position. Then stop reeling and pull the rod back up to the 1 o'clock position. Repeat this pumping action, never allowing slack in your line. Small fish shake their head in denial, which translates into a pumping action at the rod tip. Big fish power away and take line at will. Pause when the fish indicates that a run is imminent, and never reel against the drag.

Hold your ground and keep the fish under constant pressure. Be responsive to changes in direction and anticipate when the fish will tire and offer an opportunity for reeling. Don't get caught unaware when the fish decides to swim in your direction. Turn that reel until is smokes if need be. Try working the fish to the bow of the boat to avoid the motor and allow you to switch from port to starboard.

As things drag on, find an anchor point above your belt. Many fishermen work hard to sculpt their mid-section into a "pot-belly" or "donut" form, to add cushion and provide a secure footing for the pumping action that this process entails. Many of the conditioning and diet methods use to achieve this physique are risky business, but their passion for the sport is what makes them so damn attractive.

Do not lift the head of the fish out of the water until the exact moment when the landing net is being deployed. For whatever

reason, this will cause the fish to jump and flail with a renewed vigor that is most undesirable. A coordinated effort is required when that forward motion results in the fish breaching the surface of the water. Recognize when you have the advantage and finish it.

Prepare for Landing

Fishing with a buddy is most appreciated when:

1. He doesn't catch more fish than you;
2. He doesn't catch bigger fish than you;
3. And he helps you land your fish.

Value those extra set of hands. They can free a line that's caught on a cleat, pull the motor or throw an anchor. Buddy can man the net. Fish like a team.

Do not overplay fish. This starts with setting the hook again and again, when the fish is already on and small. Usually this is an excuse for a macho man to flex biceps and contort tattoos of venomous snakes. Same guy will stretch out his fifteen minutes of fame and lecture on technique and his personal attributes with the fish just hanging. And while buddy builds his brand, the fish is reduced to another prop like the mini-ponytail and the dream-catcher earring. Through all that chatter what remains is a fish that is more played out than jokes involving twelve-inch pianists. Don't be that guy. Catching the fish is proof enough.

Do not underplay fish. Take the first opportunity to land your catch, remembering that this is fishing, not netting. Don't go chasing fish three feet under the surface. It will be spooked down and the line will catch on the net, a rivet on the hull, the propeller, or tangle in the anchor rope. Don't force it because that causes men to go overboard. Fish with plenty of fight are a danger to themselves and others in the boat. To get your picture and release the fish in a hurry you need to be in control. So buddy, relax, as this is fishing after all.

If the fish is small and subdued, bring it up to shore or along the side of the boat for landing. Avoid lifting its head out of the water, as this seems to result in more of the jumping and flailing. Extend the arm that holds the rod and reach with the opposite hand to control the line and steer the fish. Reach with your arm, not your body, and grab the fish with confidence.

The toothy and spiny varieties are best served with a landing net of suitable construction and capacity. Dip the net in the water to reduce the amount of fish slime that is removed in this process. The slime shields fish from harmful bacteria and parasites. Get that net low. Avoid the net getting near the lure. Here's where an errant treble hook catches the netting a pulls the lure free from the fish. Beware of those treble hooks. Once the fish is in the net, the angler should open their bail to release the tension on the lure.

Keep it together. Perform a celebration dance and release a guttural howl, but do not ignore the wellbeing of the fish. Do not perform with the net upon the fish a series of suplexes in the style of the Iron Sheik. Do not allow the fish to languish on the hot bottom of the aluminum boat. The fish came from cool waters, so avoid any hot surfaces. Enjoy your moment. Shake your buddy's hand and take time to appreciate the beauty of fishing. Snap out of it and get that fish back in the water.

If you are not playing for keeps, the long-line release is most effective when using lures with single hooks, like a jig. Once you've seen the fish and feel satisfied with the experience, drop your rod tip and give slack line. This is catch-and-release without the fish leaving the water or being touched. If the fish is unable to free itself, grab your line, to bring fish close, and remove the hook with needle-nose pliers. Again, don't remove the fish from the water and don't touch it. Fishing like this is almost harmless.

A simple fish cradle involves a couple of four-foot boards that open and close the top of a rectangular containment net. This is the low stress method for landing trophy walleye, northern pike and muskellunge. The cradle is a riskier move than a landing net, but unless you're planning on going the traditional taxidermy route, it allows you to control those large fish in the water. The cradle is a secure place to rejuvenate a fish that might

need a few minutes before release. Angler and fish can stay calm and comfortable in the meantime. The cradle boards often have measuring tapes stretching their lengths, offering a low-impact method for competing with friends on inches.

A gaff is overkill for most circumstances and inappropriate for many fish. It takes skill to avoid being cruel with a gaff. Sticking the fish in the belly will not improve the meat. Missing the fish with the gaff and scratching the boat will not improve your relationships with friends. A gaff is useful for ice fishing, and when safety becomes an issue with monster northern pike or muskellunge. Try to hook the fish by the lower jaw, and be cautious of eyes and gills.

Off the Hook

Gain control of the fish and the situation before you attempt to remove any hooks. In these moments of excitement, rods get underfoot and fish find ways to hook you. Clear the area and delegate tasks as necessary. Unless it is food, get that fish back in the water as soon as possible. You've won the battle. Don't stress it.

Fish gloves are not just for kids and the squeamish. If necessary, they give you the confidence to get in there. Buy gloves that are puncture-resistant and that incorporate stainless steel for safety when filleting. Always wet the gloves in the water before handling the fish. Minimize contact and slime removal. Always give a thorough rinse after each fish or the gloves will soon become funkdafied in a not so fresh way.

Master the following grips:

1. Reach over the back of the fish, grab it at the shoulders, and slide your thumb and index finger forward to grip just under the gill plates. Use the palm of your hand to calm any frisky fins or spines. Be firm but don't squeeze the life out of the poor thing. This technique works for walleye, bullhead, sucker, goldeye and carp.

2. Slip your hand under the gill plate and then slide it forward towards the front of the jaw. Try not to be intrusive and don't get your fingers up in there. Use your free hand near the tail or around the belly to help support the weight of the fish. This technique works for northern pike, catfish, lake trout, and big walleye.

3. Avoid the hook. Grab the bottom jaw of the fish, turning it
   down, and rock the mouth wide open. That bottom jaw op-
   erates in a hinge-like fashion and seems to have an immobi-
   lizing quality when held ajar. Avoid the hook. This technique
   works for all sorts of bass, crappies, sunfish, perch, and drum.

With proper grip secured, use quick and decisive movements to
remove the hook. This is not a time to play around. Think of
the force that you generated with the hook set and be prepared
to exert a comparable force to remove the hook. With bone and
cartilage and such, needle-nose pliers allow you to leverage your
grip on the bend or shank of the hook. Practice a twist and jerk
motion, like shucking bottle caps. Use mouth spreaders to deal
with lockjaw in pike and walleye. If the hook is buried, consider
cutting it with wire cutters.

If you fear for your no-polish manicure or have been attacked by freshwater fish in the past, mechanical devices exist for holding the jaws of fish. As a bonus, the protective slime of the fish goes untouched, and some models have a scale built into the handle of the unit. I value my scarred and calloused hands, and almost expect to build upon the story they tell with each fishing trip. Each to his own.

If you find yourself hooked, don't first reach for the whisky. (As a general rule, you probably shouldn't have whisky within reach at all times). The booze might turn you green with nausea, and the potpourri that you will later impart shall insure the cold shoulder from health care providers and loved ones. So suck it up, push the eye down towards your body, prepare a loop of line at the bend of the hook, and yank it hard and fast. Barbless hooks make this whole process more of a joy than a chore.

First-Aid for Fish

Fish caught from thirty feet of water or more can suffer from depressurization or something similar to the bends. Eyes may bulge, blood may boil, and internal organs can expand and protrude from their mouth. This condition is familiar to Winnipeg Jets fans after a home loss. When released, depressurized fish are unable to descend and will cause a fuss before going belly up. Their best chance is to get back to the depths as soon as possible. This means releasing the fish within sixty seconds or less and offering anything from a gentle push to a football spike to help them in the downward direction.

Tournament anglers may use live wells to hold and cull fish that were caught in deep water. Once depressurization sets in, they use a needle to deflate the air bladder of the fish. You should have a good understanding of the anatomy of the fish you are targeting before attempting this technique. Fizzing harms the fish and should only be used as a last resort. Anglers should question fishing in deeper waters if they are not planning on keeping their catch.

Fish that are gut-hooked are often beyond help. With experience you will be able to judge the bite and adjust the timing of your hook set to avoid this problem. The odd time, I've had success gripping the shaft of the hook with pair of Baker Hook Out pliers and pushing the lure in, before attempting to slide it free. If the fish is dead or near death, take it home and eat it. I understand that there are situations where this doesn't seem possible, but we should make the most of what's given. If you aren't prepared to fillet the fish, then you have little business fishing.

I am well aware of the circle of life and I know that nature has many ways of consuming a dead fish. That belly up signals birds of prey and that can make for an incredible encounter or photo if luck allows. Behave as if there is a young person present who needs to be taught a lesson about life and death. Don't appear as wasteful. There are a vocal few that become disgusted and distraught at the sight of anything bloody. Consider your surroundings and govern yourself accordingly.

Worst case scenario, bag the fish, bring it back to the cabin, and stuff it in the freezer. When you are going to be away for a wee spell, throw that fish down the outhouse hole. The resulting onslaught of flies and maggots will make for a roomier and more aromatic experience when you return. Or feed it to the dog, or that raccoon who tosses your garbage each week, or the skunk that lives under something in the neighbour's yard. The only other alternative is the landfill, and this seems like a sorry-ass conclusion to a successful day of fishing.

Oh Snap!

The chase involved in fishing and photography culminates in capturing a fish or image. Both disciplines require skill, luck, knowledge of the outdoors and the determination to get into far off places on the gut feeling that nature might unfold as you imagined.

Use a floating dry box for your camera and anything else of value. There is always a first time. Fuss with the settings before you start fishing, and consider that we often fish during the low light of dawn and dusk. Keep the camera and case at ambient temperatures to avoid condensation on the lens, viewfinder and display. Position your camera within reach, because you need to be up and shooting in less than ten seconds.

Remember the fish isn't breathing, right. Show some hustle and know when to quit. Choose the best side of the fish and use gloves if necessary to get a comfortable grip. If possible, hold the fish with your palms up, using only your fingertips in the front and securing the fish with your thumbs in the back. All fish and no hands. Angle the head of the fish toward the camera, and try to expose the tail and fins. I've known people who flick the lateral line on a fish to get the spiny dorsal fin to stand up, though this practice seems questionable. Shady characters, all of 'em.

Get right up close and personal with the camera. To capture a picture of a real bull shitter, ask him to extend his chicken arms and make that fish head larger than his own (if possible). Perhaps this perspective better represents the relative brain-size. Never take photos with fish that are mocking or vulgar as these are too easy to share. Smile if you must, but refrain from any silliness that might be interpreted as disrespectful. We should not be ashamed of enjoying the good sport of fishing but fun should never be had at the expense of others.

Shoot multi-shots of the same pose like the classic horizontal for walleye and vertical for northern pike. Raise the tail-end of a channel catfish and face their charming grin into the camera. This pose can also be used to capture their iridescence and compare the beauty of your mugs. The final shots should be of the release. Get down at water level and play with the reflections. This might also be an appropriate time to shoot a quick video of the angler's reaction to the catch.

Details to include in fishing pictures: lure or bait, rod and reel, net or landing device, the boat, partners, and the scenery. If you think you're worthy of being in a magazine, you might want to make sure your PFD is visible. And if you want to avoid arrest and damaging your children forever, don't take fishing photos that glorify alcohol and tobacco. There is nothing classic about a photo of a fish drinking a beer.

Tell a story with your pictures that reflects on the fishing experience and goes beyond just the catching. Don't be a buckethead and perseverate over a list of fish to capture in the same dull pose. If you still have no clue, some ideas:

· The journey to the fishing spot
· Launching and operating the boat
· Baiting the hook and casting
· Setting the hook and fighting the fish
· Biggest fish and smallest fish
· Colour changes in close-up – fins and gills
· Stringers and shore lunch
· A group shot with any keepers
· Red skies at night
· The Unexpected

I Shall be Released

The fish has survived the battle of a lifetime. Think of the story it can tell and what bragging rights must result from surviving a meal with strings attached. "Ho hum", you say for this fish is number twenty in the boat today, all the same size. They're a bother because you're only fishing trophies (same bait and presentation though). This encounter may be the only time this fish is caught. Make it special. Appreciate the variations in colouring, check the eyes and gills and body. Think of what it does to you to hold a wild thing. That should never become ho hum.

Length is the measure of a trophy. Be accurate and consistent by using a bump board. The head of the fish is pushed up against a fixed edge and the length measurement is taken at the tail end. The fish lies flat and your hands are free to control the situation and administer high-fives. If you perform a girth measurement

(the distance around the fattest part), there are charts available to estimate the weight of your fish. Affix a sticker or old measuring tape to the side of your boat to accomplish the same. Record your trophies by scratching lengths and dates into the exterior of your tackle box.

The long-line release is most humane, but we can't live in the past. Now grab your fish by the tail and slide your other hand from the gill plate down to the belly. Large fish carry more weight in that area than your average comic con attendee. Fish are used to the belly support provided by the water. Get low to the water and make sure the weight of your boat is balanced before reaching over the gunwale.

Get comfortable so that you can hold that position and the fish. It may take seconds to release a fish or it may take minutes, so settle in. You need to stay with them until they are able to swim away under their own power. Use a gentle sawing motion to bring water through the gills. This should be slow and easy, back and forth, to mimic a breathing pattern. Angle the head down and let the fish kick a little before letting go of the tail. Wash up. Pat yourself on the back.

At stage in this process, if the fish is uncooperative and as a result your ego may be bruised or your body otherwise harmed, please control your urge to lash out. The fish did not intend to inflict any damage and did in no way conspire to bring your reputation into question. Take a deep breath, release, and repeat. No need for acrobatics, extended free falls, or skipping of fish.

Killing in the Name of

This should be difficult. Pause to say thanks. Reflect on those who will eat this fish and enjoy improved health as a result. Never kill something without good reason. Feel the power to kill at will and don't allow it to be satisfying.

Stringers and live wells keep the fish until you are ready to get eating or packing the freezer. I've seen stringers of fish filleted by the propeller. I've seen stringers of fish eaten by mink. Don't forget the fish.

You may need to visualize a particular scene to do the deed, and I don't mean to make light of the situation, but here are a few suggestions:

1. The politician who smokes all the dope for himself;
2. The winter driver who thinks it's safer to drive 30 klicks in a 60 zone;

3. The car thief responsible for the loss of Huey Lewis and the News "Sports" cassette.

A fish bat was a project in our Grade 8 woodworking class. Each week, we would make a new bat and stage attacks on each other during the bus ride. The proper term for this killing technique is percussive stunning. This method works best for small and medium-sized fish. Hold the fish against a hard and stable surface, and strike the brain to cause blunt force trauma. Two quick hits is good practice. Be prepared for blood splatter and the commotion from when life leaves the body.

Spiking puts a scratch awl to use. It looks like a screwdriver but has a sharpened and/or pointed tip and the handle is shaped to rest in the heel of your palm. Easy does it there, tough guy. Use your fillet board to avoid puncturing pedestal seats or the leg of your Minnesota Vikings Zubaz. The idea is to detroy the brain with a push and stir motion.

Where's My Mule?

You are late, really late. Fishing was so good that you ignored the nagging voice and that's understandable (at least, to me it is). Now you have to haul ass to get home in time for something or other, and cleaning that stringer of fish up proper will put at risk your sex life and place of residence. What were you thinking? I know. Now, better think quick.

Do not transport live fish. They might find their way into your waterbed and interrupt a good night's sleep. Do not store whole fish in bucket of water, as this causes all sorts of slime to build up that can make for dangerous cleaning. Instead, wrap each fish in newspaper (funnies or obituaries) and put on ice. Transport using these silver cooler bags that are relatively inexpensive and have no bulk. However, chances are you brought a cooler and it is empty by the end of the day. Drain whatever slurry of liquids remain in the bottom and avoid cross-contamination.

When you get home, unwrap each bundle, filet the fish, and wrap up the waste for disposal. Even if you have your limit, this type of self-contained cleanliness will allow you to maintain access to a kitchen and its precious contents. Wash your fish in cool water and store in large freezer bags or plastic containers. Separate your catch into family-sized portions, surround the filets with water, and seal. The ice helps protect the filets from freezer burn and seems to help them keep longer. For bachelors without a chest freezer, filets can be frozen separate on a cookie sheet and later transferred to a freezer bag. Always date your catch and rotate your freezer stock. Waste not, want not.

Chapter 8

In High Seas or in Low Seas

How to Drown – Pt. 3

Friend, are you a piss-tank? Do you believe that peeing from the boat should be celebrated? Your actions may result in you pissing on your own grave. And I understand that you might find a certain brotherhood in relieving yourself in unusual places, but from the boat is not what I consider best practice.

(To protect their identities, I have changed the names of the characters involved.)

When Dad's friend ventured to raise the level and temperature of Stonehouse Lake from the bow of a sixteen-foot aluminum boat, Dad sensed the cultural importance of what he was about to witness. With VHS camera, he captured a cherub of a man realizing his true calling, but then faltering, and we all know what happens next.

Despite the buoyancy of their banana leaf hats and Churchill cigars, they spilled overboard, sank and sometime later resurfaced. Dad recalls coming-to after being knocked out, about ten feet below the surface with the bubbles from his nose and mouth now slowing. All was lost. Yet, with their remaining wits, they chose to stay with the upturned boat, holding onto the gunnel rail to save energy. There were a couple of crazed attempts to flip the boat over from in the water. And they tried to swim the boat to shore, but let's blame that on shock and not further stupidity.

From a distance, I noticed a silver flash (from the bottom hull) instead of Lund red (along the topside). I remember the dramatic rescue; it was like a scene from *Miami Vice* where Crockett and Tubbs thwart the smugglers while Phil Collins rocks a drum solo. The Dads were red-faced. We towed them to shore, whereupon the same character declared he was going to finish what he started. He faltered again, and smacked his head on a rock. We later learned that his enthusiasm for orange juice that morning was not brought on by fear of scurvy, but also coincided with a fair dint in our vodka stocks. Surprise surprise.

Friend, when nature calls, pay it a visit. Take the boat to shore and mark that spot with something of substance and your creation. Declare the wilds conquered for the forces of good, if you must. Or if you are not one for grand gestures, maybe just drink less in the boat (not that I'm telling you what to do, of course).

Please also consider what's readily available: a bailing can or funnel, a length of bilge pump hose, tape or clamps, and with some modifications your "system" can make due. If you need this tip illustrated, you have no business setting foot in a boat. And while I would argue that such a system lacks the dignity and charm of a trip to shore, dear reader, I pass no judgment.

How to Commit Suicide by Boat

The first outboard motor that I commanded was a 2.2 horsepower made by Johnson. They were forward-thinking folks back in the '50s, so this motor didn't have reverse. To propel the old tin boat backward, you spun the engine right around, and the tiller handle then pivoted forward. The boat would jerk, the motor would rear up, and most of the time that was just the kind of excitement I was after. Got a taste of freedom in that boat, but the point being: we have progressed.

Outboard motors are now equipped with safety lanyards that shut off the engine when disengaged, if you are thrown from the boat, for instance. Otherwise, a boat without a skipper tends to travel in a perpetual circle carving you up and knocking you senseless. Consider as an alternative, attaching the safety lanyard clip to your ragged jean shorts, cut-off sweatpants or what have you. If you fail, so does the engine. But if you forget, just hope that you get it good on that first pass around, because it only gets uglier.

JT's On the Water Essentials

1. Large Dry Bag
2. Floating Dry Box in Blaze Orange
3. Tarp – for unscheduled overnight adventures and spontaneous poncho making
4. Rope – a length for towing and anchoring, small lengths for docking
5. Bungee cords – keeps it all in the boat
6. Space blankets – they fold small and reflect heat
7. Hippie blanket – bulky, but warm in case of emergency
8. Camp Hatchet – doubles as a hammer, and for self-defence
9. Leatherman Wave – for channeling Richard Dean Anderson
10. Traditional Chinese scissors – for cutting bait
11. Berkley 14" Digital Lip Grip – built-in scale for friendly competitions
12. Headnets/Thermacell – or them bugs'll drive you mad
13. Hand Towels – not the ones that your better half puts out for company
14. Whistle or Fog Horn – in case you need to draw more attention to your mistakes
15. Compass/Maps/GPS – do not rely on electronic devices, they are not your master
16. More Fire – matches, lighter, fire steel, cotton balls saturated in petroleum jelly
17. Duct tape – the real stuff
18. Signal mirror – to look death in the face
19. Toilet paper – leaves of three, let them be
20. Moist Toilettes – because of how you eat

21. Garbage bags – commercial grade will hold water
22. Rubber Net – the standard size with a basket-style net
23. Landing Net – jumbo because you never know
24. PFD's – top quality, a variety of sizes, accessible, extras on hand
25. Whatever else the law requires and allows

How to Drown – Pt. 4

Tossing out the anchor seems basic. It is far from basic. I set an anchor that broke free one night during a storm in Prince William Sound. We came very close to wrecking a fishing skiff and two sailboats. (Serves them right, trusting a boy from the prairies). I also set an anchor but gave it too much slack line. We awoke the next morning with skeg on bottom, stuck at forty-five degrees with funhouse floors until the tides turned.

Buddy tells a story of fishing on Lake Winnipeg with a cinder block anchor and the rope laying in a coil on the floor of the boat. The first mistake he made was tossing the anchor out the side. Always throw the anchor from the bow. If the rope comes up short, it will cause the bow to dive, but it won't cause the boat to tip. In this instance, Buddy's leg was the reason the rope came up short. He dove into the opposite gunnel to stop the boat from tipping. The boat reared up hard and he lived to tell the story.

Other Buddy learned a similar lesson on the Red River near Lockport. The flow was raging that day, yet so were the channel cats. They knew from experience to avoid where the river owns you, but still push up against the locks and set anchor. Here, Buddy throws it and the line loops around his wrist. Other Buddy slams the motor into reverse and dives across the boat to grab his hand. That anchor bites and the rope tightens, and Buddy would have experienced the worst snag of his life. There is good reason, why in previous generations the most successful hunters and fishers were revered. It can be challenging work.

With the proper knife in hand you might have a fighting chance after you hit the water. Keep that knife in a belt holster or in your front pocket at all times when you are in a boat. I choose a tactical knife with a serrated blade and spring-assist opener that allows one-hand deployment. Find a knife you can trust and practise for emergencies. As a bonus, tactical knives inspire confidence, look cool, and provide hours of opening enjoyment with only minor lacerations and the odd puncture wound. A case study in first aid.

Never Leave Home Without It

Timberline Tactical Knife

· 3.25" serrated tanto blade
· 4.25" when folded, slim with belt clip
· Attached a lanyard in case of a bear fight.
· Keeps the knife close when fighting with fists.

How to Hit Rock Bottom

I will fish until I die. May it be a good long life because fishing puts more back into you than it takes out. But I seldom wear a personal floatation device in the boat, and never along the shoreline. (Do as I say, not as I do). Suppose I had the life sucked out of me by those orange keyholes, and I've shrugged off the straight jackets ever since. If you grow up around boats, dangers are taken as a given, and later flirted with. It is a way of life (or death). I am over-confident in my ability to swim long distances. I think I can withstand KO blows with a Homeresque sense of poise and style. We all sink.

You should have lengths of rope tied to the bow and stern; rope that is not tangled and that has a good knot at the end. These lines can be thrown to someone in distress in rough water.

Don't trust the seat cushion. At some point, your fat ass crushed all the buoyancy. You will tire easily when treading water without a life jacket. Consider fishing geek chic, with a snappy pair of suspenders that disguise a PFD with CO_2 and manual inflation. If you can't swim, wear one of these and be at ease. For fishing early season and up north, I like the Floater jacket. In the cold, clothing is layered and maximum warmth and buoyancy is required. Remember, knives can be used to cut weight.

How to Drop $100K

The boat show is a great place to start. Winter is annoying by the end of February, and summer is a wash of endless sunshine and waters turbulent with fish. Used boats are still crowded into barns or resting under the snowpack, while all things shiny harken the renewal that spring embodies. There is reason for optimism. It don't hurt to look, does it?

Booth after booth of tournament boats in metallic-flake paints, pimped with pedal throttles, trim paddles and insane electronics. For the look of a gangster rapper, add the trolling motor remotes worn around your neck like medallions. The cowlings are open to see how the engine will sound (something like testosterone). There is power to spare. And now that fourteen-foot runabout doesn't seem that badass.

Never owned a boat before in your life? Here's a lark, how about a twenty-two foot pontoon boat with a 200 horsepower outboard. It's perfect if you don't want to have to leave the living room to drag the kid around in a tube. There's a compact hi-fi to spin your Lawrence Welk sides, and a little prep area for the squeeze cheese and crackers. It is a substantial purchase, more than you could have imagined, and that's just the beginning.

There are some steep sections of the Trans-Canada Highway coming from the prairies into the Canadian Shield. Don't be

fooled by the spoilers, hood vents and ground effects, those mini-vans are not so powerful. For some, it may take a couple of transmissions to realize that you now have to upgrade your tow vehicle. Cha-ching. Add the extra insurance cost to that of the boat and trailer.

And you can't just tie-up a 5,000 pound boat to the dock and expect that, hell or high water, it will be there in the morning. With a waterfront cabin, that means a hydraulic boatlift with steel canopy roof or maybe even a boathouse. Driving a boat of this size takes more finesse when docking, but you don't know that because you never driven a boat. (But you have your boat operator's card!). First time out, you come in hot and damaged goods. At $100K and counting, what started as a runabout is fast becoming a sinking ship. There's a good reason most anglers you see are driving a simple sixteen-foot tin boat.

Chapter 9

The Fishing Outfit

Function versus Fashion

If you like to dress like a fool, clear a place in your heart and closet for fishing gear. You will no longer be a poseur when you wear your vest with all the pockets. Instead, you'll be that guy who has to explain what each pockets holds. As a general rule, be prepared for the worst or be prepared to suffer in silence. If you're cold, put on a wool sweater. And shut up about it. There's nothing to complain about when you are fishing. Nothing. When fishing, other shit just don't matter.

Neil Young sings about a time when "people wore what they had on". Fishing is accepting in the same way, but you must be authentic in denim, flannel, and wool. In their younger days afield, the good spirits of my grandfathers seasoned some of the finest pieces in my wardrobe. With a dash of dank and hint of musty, these natural fabrics helped nurture a thick skin. Baked over a fire each evening, the funk fortifies the wearer with the powers of antiquity. Gear is necessary if it keeps you fishing longer.

The fashion police are not welcome on the water. Allow lesser individuals to be preoccupied trying to coordinate their Love Boat-inspired shirts with pleated khakis and flip-flops. Out of principle, avoid anything yoga-inspired and manufactured from an oil sands by-product. Get a good fishing sweat going, and that new smell becomes perma-stink over a weekend. And camp life doesn't allow for the fine fabric to be washed with ambrosia on gentle and dried on a bed of baby's breath.

I notice the growing popularity of "fancy shirts" that compete for corporate logos and garish graphics. If you are a tournament angler, you've earned the right to sell space on the seat of your pants, if that is what your audience demands. My guess is that most of these guys have a better chance of securing sponsorship from manufacturers of bacon, toothpicks and toilet bowl

cleaner. We all can dream, but let's tame the theatrics. I understand the need to display your shore-cred, but if you're that particular, take up fly fishing.

Put a Lid on It

"Grass doesn't grow on a busy street", at least that's what I tell the kids. That hairless patch on my crown is known as the "cool spot", for the frequent gasps of awe and cries of envy that it elicits. If you are so fortunate as to have undergone this rebirth of sorts, celebrate your achievement, and preserve its milky glow rather than allow the sun to create a spotted print referred to as the "Monty Burns". Headwear is optional, but if you know what's good for you, bring a hat. It helps keep the bugs off and the brim can save your face from errant treble hooks. Variety is the spice of life, so please consider your options:

- The natural choice is a hat made from the broad leaves of tropical plants and often accessorized with fruit appliques or exotic
chicken feathers. Also in this category are cowboy hats that
tumbled into your life, and once served as residential quarters
for a seabird, mollusk, and crab. In emergency circumstances,
these hats can be smoked or used as fire starter.
- Fishing has a special place for hats will vulgar slogans and
mesh backs. Novelty hats that incorporate the head and tail
of a stuffed fish have also proven timeless. Choose these hats
with caution for they often transform the wearer into a know-
it-all that stumbles and slurs.

- Desert hats combine a ball cap with two hankies that cover
your neck and create a mullet-like aura. Found often in a
checkerboard print, these fashion treasures should be secured
with a roach clip to your Quiet Riot t-shirt, or a gust of wind
will find your magnetism reduced during the next snowball
at the roller rink.
- Hats that hold beers draw attention. In fact, any article of
clothing that advertises alcohol could be removed from the

picture. I know for many people from Winnipeg, this excludes 75 percent of their wardrobe, leaving only neon tank tops and jam shorts. I'm just sayin'.

· Tilley hats invite beat downs from roving youth-at-risk. I also don't like Tilley hats. They seem to trap hot air and cause the head to swell. And assholes wear them.

· Bandanas are somewhat acceptable. Good varieties invoke patriotism and express a love for explosions and flames. Bad varieties encourage gang violence, swashbuckling, and swaying like Axl Rose. Significant facial hair of the salt and pepper variety is a prerequisite.

When it Rains it Pours

Those who mean business choose Grundens and Xtratufs. It's the Alaskan power suit, when complemented by other survival accessories like well-crafted beards and beers.

Grunden rainsuits are made for the North Sea by badass Swedes. This is gear meant for catching fish; so don't ask about the features. My jacket doesn't even have pockets. But it is waterproof and has a neoprene inner cuff. And this is the part where I talk about some cool new fabric that breathes and is waterproof and makes you appear awesome. Bullshit! I like an orange jacket and green pants. You're visible but not chain gang. Other reasons why the rain don't bother me:

1. There are no bells and whistles to get tangled in gear or lake bottom;
2. PVC don't hold the smell of fish slime and stink bait;
3. They are easy to remove if you get tossed into the drink;
4. They survive the careless consumption of wine-dipped cigarellos;

5. They won't melt when you get too close to your shore lunch fire;

6. They last almost as long as a good pair of underwear.

Save the penny loafers for preppies and the boat shoes for yuppies. I prefer the Xtratuf boots that are worn by the hell raisers who brave the Bering Sea. I've slept in these boots aboard a sailboat named Taku. Comfy and they seal around the ankle to negate casual booters and rough patches. If you have plans for the evening, simply roll down the cuff and they become the Alaskan dress boot. It was always a good sign when your date shows up wearing Xtratufs.

What you need:

· Grunden Harvestor 44 Hooded Jacket
· Grunden Harvestor 116 Bib Pant
· Xtratuf 15" Legacy boots - Uninsulated
· Ranpro Cape Ann Sou'wester Hat
· Cabela's Dry Bag

Chapter 10

Where Do the Children Play?

Where to Begin

I call you dumbass because I want you to feel like you belong. Fishing is inclusive. All are welcome regardless of age, education, income, or level of coordination. There are no written or practical tests that require a passing grade to earn your fishing licence. There are no try-outs, hazing or over-aggressive coaches. Fishing doesn't require physical fitness, special ability or any particular intelligence. Fishing is for dumbasses, and that's beauty.

Fishing is fun whether you are catching or not. Take a listen to nature, when all other devices are sleeping. It may take an hour or two for your brain to adjust, maybe a day or two depending on your habit of screen time. A quiet understanding is found while fishing. With practice, it becomes a mindset that you can access when necessary (especially at work). Fishing can affect your daily rhythm.

Age is not an obstacle. Young people have their eyesight to thread fine lines through hook eyes, and they have the agility to work a section of river with a dry fly. Because of desk jobs and marriage, old farts are well practiced in the art of sitting put, waiting out long periods of silence, all the while ready for any hint of action. And there are fish that suit the pace of both stereotypes. Rappel rock faces to access remote mountain pools for native trout or fish dough baits for freshwater drum from the loveseat in the bed of your pick-up. Either way, the element of the unknown and the thrill of the hunt can keep you feeling young.

The goal of fishing is not achievement in the sense that one triumphs over another. An education is demonstrated by how you approach fishing and what you take away from the experience. The spirit of the outdoors awaits those who partake in its rituals. Don't be afraid to make mistakes and believe that your dumb luck will turn on the next cast.

Excel at fishing even if you come from a modest background. There are no upfront fees and no salespeople will visit your home. Forget expert coaches, dry-land training, and special diets, you need only to arrive. Your average person lives near to a place that holds trophy fish, and this is especially true if you can gain perspective on what constitutes a trophy.

Be a spazz, a klutz or just plain gangly. Fishing as a solitary pursuit allows you to find confidence at your pace. Nothing makes you feel more alive than catching a wild animal and consuming its flesh. Fishing is unpredictable and it is that simple. You can never tell what a day of fishing holds.

How to Corrupt Young Minds

Don't get yourself in a state. I am known to be more than enthusiastic. This joie de vivre is sometimes mistaken for volatility or "anger issues". (Screw you. I will eat your children). As a father, I am nothing but a model of patience and restraint. Fishing with the kids seemed as easygoing as the whistle from Andy of Mayberry, at least until that day I found myself in a pit of blue-streaked rage.

The river level drops in the late season exposing mud flats and steep cut banks. I know the challenges these conditions bring to landing fish, but the kids talked me into it. This spot was flooded in May, now our rod holders were jammed all cockeyed in the cracked earth. We caught a few bullheads and a stonecat, and had no problems hoisting them up and expediting their departure.

Take it serious when you take on fishing with the kids. My lesson in catch-and-release with a channel cat turned, when I focused more on lecturing than the task at hand. After hook removal, the fish slipped from my grasp, and careened over the edge of the bank to great surprise and rapturous attention. A kid would describe it like those Duke Boys' cliffhangers, stopped mid-frame as Waylon Jennings quips about the rarity of such a thing in Hazzard County. When the action continued, that catfish half buried in the muck below was an awful pity flopping there all helpless like. From the look on my daughter's face, I knew that Daddy was about to take one for the fishing team.

Trouble progressed with each step in pursuit and soon I ended up to my Daisy Dukes in the thick stuff and that catfish croaking still out of reach. This abyss brought my resolve into question. If only the mud could swallow my words, for the kids' vocabulary exploded that day. Unable to kick with anger, I punched the air with stinging combinations, while frozen with madness and from the mud that enveloped 50 percent of my surface area and growing. I reimagined Dorf on Fishing. It was a profane adaptation.

Where were the assholes on jet skis that always buzz the shore? Their wake could pull the fish out to safety. And I'd have

a precious few inches to drown myself. Where were the chatty old men with basset hounds all in matching sweaters? Free me from this horror with a swift tug from your cane or leash. Or please, bore me to death with another health-related story! How long before a murder of crows cackles their lunch call and I am reduced to nothing, man? Never soon enough.

In my mind, I was alone and empty. The kids have learned to keep quiet in these not infrequent types of unfortunate circumstances, while at the same time refraining from hearing a thing (and so these episodes shall never be repeated). Through the fury and after that trapped feeling wore off, I chose this opportunity to demonstrate to the kids my raw power and blind aggression. Wearing the pained grimace of Han Solo in carbonite, I wretched from the Land of Slurp the legs that no longer felt as my own. Dirty and ashamed, my crawl up the bank provided the kids with a visual reference for just how low their father can be.

I'm still mad at myself for the mess I made of that fishing adventure. How many "normal" days of fishing will it take for the family to forget that self-implosion? My wife is keeping count. She'll let me know when the damage is reversed. Recognize that these moments make memories, good or bad, but always telling. Laugh at yourself, the sooner the better, for that is the character that fishing brings about. Now grow up.

How to Play God

For over twenty years, I pursued the northern crayfish. In the early spring, drawn into the frigid waters for sport. Along the shoreline and near the docks and ramps, I would spot and stalk, their brilliant blue claws exposing their position in the sand next to or under rocks. Crayfish scurry backwards, raising a cloud of silt to disguise the path of their retreat. I kept my catch in a bucket until I judged their continued incarceration inhumane. I set them free in the afternoon and rounded them up the next morning, all summer long.

Never that many, but enough to catch a few each time you ventured out with the snorkeling equipment and sturdy nets from the tropical fish shop. Other methods include using raw meat or cat food as an attractant. The hot dog on a string technique was popular on Lake of the Woods where the crib docks hold them in numbers. One banner day at Falcon Lake, we caught over twenty northern crayfish and served them fire-roasted with hot butter. Mum has never let us do that again.

And then one day, I find a rusty crayfish in Falcon Lake. Their claws dwarf that of the northern, and their disposition is that of fight rather than flee. Rusty crayfish push the northern crayfish out of their hiding spots making them more vulnerable to the small-mouth bass. Rusty crayfish are bullies and baby makers, enough so that they destroyed the northern crayfish over two summers.

Rusty crayfish were likely introduced into Falcon Lake by anglers who transported their bait from one lake to another. Nice move fellas. Now at the lake, my kids catch over one hundred rusty crayfish a day. They are tickled but I'm a bit creeped out. I am convinced the rusties are the reason why the fish are avoiding artificial lures. Falcon Lake is not dead, but time will tell of the impact of this introduction.

Aquatic invasive species also include mussels, waterfleas, minnows, reeds and weeds. Familiarize yourself with the culprits. Manitoba Conservation and Water Stewardship recommends the following course of action to anglers:

1. Clean

Clean and inspect watercraft, trailer, aircraft, and all water-based equipment and gear. Remove all plants, animals, mud. Rinse using high pressure (>250 psi) and extremely hot tap water – 50°C (120°F) for at least two minutes; or 60°C (140°F) for at least 10 seconds.

2. Drain

Drain all water from watercraft, equipment, and gear including the motor, livewell, bilge, bait buckets, and totes before transporting.

3. Dry

Dry watercraft, trailer, and all water-based gear and equipment for at least five days in the hot sun, 18 days in the spring/fall, or freeze for three days (if rinsing is not available).

4. Dispose

Dispose of unwanted live bait and worms in the trash, and dump all water from bait buckets and totes on land away from any waterbody.

All That's Sacred Comes From Youth

This book ain't for kids, fuck. Spare the rod and spoil the child. Or spare the child and spoil them with a nice rod. Or Rod's spare child is spoiled. (Please excuse me if I misquoted your god.) Point being, don't hit your kids, stupid, and especially not with this book or a fishing rod.

There are plenty of kids who want to learn how to fish. And there are those labelled "youth-at-risk" who deserve our attention instead of judgment. Try not to let your habits get in the way. Take comfort that a fishing trip trumps any Christmas gift, birthday surprise, or special event. On or near the water, we make those childhood memories that ground us in the outdoors and this country. Fishing might be your only good habit, so teach your children well and hope it balances out the rest. Always have a game plan, explain the variables (weather, work, level of patience), and emphasize the importance of just spending time outdoors.

Undersell the whole experience. Remain vague about the fine details of the casting and hook setting and fish fighting variety, and instead reinforce the team effort. Make no promises of fish. Weave stories about the one that got away, and relive every man-overboard and filet knife mishap. Fear and apprehension is to be expected, if not encouraged. Kids should always wear a life jacket near water until long after they are skilled swimmers. Ability is not the biggest obstacle; it's more the resilience to remain calm and clear-headed in a time of discomfort and uncertainty. Other fishing essentials include eye protection, bug repellent, sunscreen, and constant attention.

If you have never fished before, become a kid again. Allow yourself to feel that sense of wonder and amazement, wild with surprise when you pull a fish from the water. Hold close the proof of your progress, and that it and you are alive. Teach your children how to learn their lessons and laugh at their trials. Without the judgment from the team or other parents and without the pressure to be the best, you find motivation alone and in search of some indefinable force. There are fishing partners, more often than fishing teams, but the idea is the same. You work the water together and share in the successes. Be prepared to laugh at yourselves. Choose your partner well, because these bonds tend to last a lifetime.

If you are a master angler, take a step back and deep breath. No time to go macho. Pass the rod to the child and allow them to lose fish. Yes, I am suggesting that we allow a child to fail. They will learn to appreciate the struggle and take pride when they see the fish. Don't build the expectation that every fish hooked will be landed. And don't assume that every kid shares your fire for competition. Relax and remember your first fish. Leave the child be and they might teach you something.

Fishing is perfect for the parent who doesn't want their kids to compete (lose, in particular). Because fishing will help undo those best intentions by exposing the child and parent to situations where there is no plan, no hope and the safety police aren't answering. These situations should not be avoided, rather navigated with caution. Take on the challenge of fishing to prepare your children for the world they'll inherit.

Problem with kids these days is that their concentration sucks. It's the video games, right. They are all obsessed with the blood and gore, the danger, and the unexpected. Games reward repetitive motor skills and stubborn persistence. Let's indulge that mindset, as today's parents do, and remind kids that real fishing has all of the above qualities. Fishing also involves the sitting and snacks that they are all too familiar with, but also cool water, fresh air, and wilderness. Fishing is relaxing without the mind-numbing side effects.

Game over. Steal from the hands of children and curb-stomp the screens. Stop the irreversible damage on our culture. Frame these devices as an educational tool, and kids will be happy to go outside to avoid them. Reward your children with more time, threaten to throw it away, and let this ware become their all-in-one friend, confidant, and caregiver. They learn to play games with their lives. Fishing is a cellular dead zone and WiFi cold spot, as far as I am concerned. Perhaps the rod manufacturers can conspire (like they haven't already) to implant scrabblers into the handles of fishing poles.

I know this is falling on deaf ears (thanks to the iPod), but as these kids become more immersed in a virtual environment, they lose touch, and it becomes easier for them to be complicit in destroying Earth. We must rely on the strong backs and minds of young people to make the traditions of fishing and conservation their own. Shoreline cleanup efforts and habitat restoration

projects introduce kids to the idea that they can change the world with their own two hands. Catching fish for dinner starts the conversation around the table and feeds on the value of personal experience. Fishing may be radicalized, if we rely on computers to teach our children. Here's how we change our course:

1. *Half-hour to start* – build from there in fifteen-minute increments (parents recognize that your enthusiasm may wane before your child's, and that's okay).

2. *Fish from shore* – go simple and cheap with bobbers, split shot, and small single hooks to minimize time between tangles.

3. *Assorted live bait* – kids play with the wrapping paper instead of their toy, so get minnows and crawlers and some other critter, or better yet, catch your own.

4. *Tackle box Q&A* – give the child permission to look and touch, provided they listen to your fish stories and put things back where they found them.

5. *Two rods + Two kids + One adult* – this is maximum capacity and should only be attempted by the experienced. And yes, that means you're not fishing (deal with it).

6. *Explore the shore* – collect bugs, pick berries, smell flowers and take notice of every little detail. Compare with your subsequent adventures.

7. *Make it a Picnic* – reinforce the ideals of healthy living and stop funding child obesity, bring candied salmon or sushi, or cook by fire.

8. *Catch fish!* – don't matter the size or variety, wild versus stocked, native versus invasive, try for one fish. No luck; fake a bite, stage a fight, lose like a sport.

9. *Keep fish* – open up that belly, watch the eyes widen, involve their hands in the process, and while you have their attention, give thanks.

ACKNOWLEDGEMENTS

Love to Carol, Jackson and Gloria for eating what I put on the table and for giving the writer a warm place to call home. Thank you to all the great folks at Great Plains Publishing for inviting me along for this adventure. Much respect to all the friends who shared a story, picture, or opinion: Darrin Bohonis, Bob Bonnefoy, Jerry Kruzcek, Dylan Fries, Don Lamont, Louis Lauzon, Todd Longley, Craig McDougall, Maurice Mierau, Andrea Munster, Jonny Peake, Michael Roberts, Michael Sanders, and Nathan Terin. Special thanks to members of the Hastings School Fishing Club (circa 1985): Brett Adam, Cam Barth, Steve Bolton, Cam Coleman, Dan Gobeil, Scott Hutton, and Colin Rodrigue.

I have volunteered for Fish Futures Inc. for over twenty years. Our goal is to get more kids fishing. Learn more about our programs at www.fishfutures.net.